Outlines

ARTHUR RIMBAUD

Other Books by Benjamin Ivry

Maurice Ravel
(Everyman / Knopf, 1999)

Paradise for the Portuguese Queen: poems
(Orchises, 1998)

Francis Poulenc
(Phaidon, 1996)

ARTHUR RIMBAUD

BENJAMIN IVRY

Absolute Press

First published in 1998 by Absolute Press
Scarborough House, 29 James Street West,
Bath, Somerset, England BA1 2BT
Tel: 01225 316013 Fax: 01225 445836
email sales@absolutepress.demon.co.uk

Distributed in the United States of America and Canada by
Stewart, Tabori and Chang
115 West 18th Street, New York, Ny 10011

Cover and text Design by Ian Middleton

Printed by The Cromwell Press, Melksham
Covers printed by Devenish and Co. Bath

ISBN1 899791 55 8

Contents

Acknowledgements

Thanks are due for advice and encouragement to Richard Howard and Marie Ponsot, masterful poets and translators both, Sidney Buckland, Harold and Carol Rolfe, Martha Hollander and Jonathan Bumas, Charity Hume, Jinsey Dauk, Grace Schulman, James Marrow, Kenneth Schneider, Irwin Gonshak, Ricardo Morin; in Paris, Fernando Arrabal, Yannick Guillou, Jeannine and Gérard Worms, Hu Ying-Chieh, Philippe Joly, David and Marie-Thérèse Lieberman, Carolyn Kizer and John Marshall Woodbridge. Thanks at Absolute Press to the publisher Jon Croft and series editor Nick Drake, designer Ian Middleton, Christine Leech and photo researcher Matt Inwood.

Preface

'Still, it's sad to think that present-day French poetry came out of this coupling of pederasts.'
Colonel Godchot, an early biographer of Rimbaud.

The Frenchman Arthur Rimbaud (1854–1891) is renowned for having expanded ideas of what language can do in poetry, although he stopped writing at about the age of twenty. With Paul Verlaine, a great lyric poet, he made one of the most famous and notorious gay couples in history although they only lived together for about two years. V&R's relationship was notorious because it was often violent, including sado-masochistic routines and a much-publicized shooting incident. A new study of the gay elements in Rimbaud's life and work is needed because his sexuality has been much discussed, often badly. No writer on Rimbaud can ignore the V&R relationship, but even today some follow the opinion of the biographer Pierre Petitfils that he was not gay, but a heterosexual who participated in painfully willed sexual 'experiments' to become a seer. Yet there is abundant evidence in poems that Rimbaud enjoyed his gayness and no comparable evidence that he was seriously attracted to women. There have been many other myths as listed by the critic René Etiemble, including Rimbaud the seer, the thug, the Catholic, the Communard, the homosexual, and so on. Books have been devoted to each of these identities and although the biographer Marcel Coulon frankly discussed his sexuality in the 1920s, it was not until 1937 that Robert Goffin linked the poetry's beauty to the poet's gayness. He wrote, 'An individual's poetic quality is a function of his gift of love', thus stating what needs reestablishing today, that Rimbaud was 'from his earliest youth, an exceptional being dedicated somatically and psychically to homosexuality'. What does it matter? Why categorize, as a liberal friend recently asked me, explaining why she was opposed in principle to anthologies of gay writing. Unfortunately, denying gay culture is still a frequent means of suppressing the people whose culture it is: it was only in the mid-1990s that authoritative survey volumes were published about homosexuality in Japanese and Arabic literature, and even then the author of the Japanese study, an American academic, stated that colleagues warned him that his career would be ruined if he published. The denial of gay culture should be opposed as willful ignorance by all those who care about culture, but sadly such is not yet the case.

This book's focus will be more biographical than critical in response to attempts to force Rimbaud into 'a heterosexual vision of the world which was certainly not his', as the critic Steve Murphy wrote. Particular attention will be paid to his affair with Verlaine and his presumed relationships with Germain Nouveau, Jean-Louis Forain, and Ernest Cabaner. A final chapter investigates his impact on the lives and works of other artists. Based on original sources, this book is nevertheless indebted to the biographers Enid Starkie, Pierre Petitfils, Vernon Underwood and Jean-Luc Steinmetz, and the critics André Guyaux, Louis Forestier, Cecil Hackett, Antoine Fongaro, Jean-Pierre Giusto, Antoine Adam, and Steve Murphy. (see the bibliography).

RIMBAUD PHOTOGRAPHED BY ETIENNE CARJAT

Before Verlaine: 1854–1871

Jean-Nicolas-Arthur Rimbaud was born on October 20, 1854 in Charleville, in the northern Ardennes region of France. He was the second son of a career soldier, Frédéric Rimbaud, and his wife Marie-Catherine-Vitalie Cuif. Captain Rimbaud had served in Algeria and the Crimea and by the time Arthur was six he had left the family home for good, driven away by his difficult wife. The four Rimbaud children – Arthur's elder brother Frédéric, born in 1853 and sisters Vitalie, born in 1858, and Isabelle, born in 1860 – all suffered under the stiff French matriarch. The Captain died in Dijon in 1878 without seeing his family again. Madame Rimbaud rented her farm out to peasant workers for decades, until even they moved on. To drive away French peasants, among nature's most sedentary creatures, took an unusual talent for repelling people. No portrait survives of either Rimbaud parent, which was unusual for a time when even humble families commissioned them, but the father had vanished and the mother did not encourage sentimentality. The Captain, after his service in Algeria, took a particular interest in Arab matters and among the unpublished manuscripts he left behind were an Arabic-French dictionary and a translation of the Koran. Arthur would take an interest in these later in life; but like all prodigies, he cannot be explained by his parents, teachers or surroundings: he was a self-starter, writing travel stories and adventures.

Arthur was a small, brown-haired, pale boy with strikingly beautiful eyes and his childhood friend Ernest Delahaye described his 'very contractile blue irises ... in a double blue in which the zones, darker and lighter, got bigger or blended in moments of revery and when thinking intensely. When he searched or saw into the unknown, and if his mental vision went far, the eyelids drew closer in a feline way. The long silky eyelashes trembled lightly, while the head retained an attentive immobility.' Elsewhere Delahaye wrote about his 'eyes of pale blue irradiated with dark blue – the loveliest eyes I've seen – with an expression of bravura ready to sacrifice everything when he was serious, of a childish sweetness, exquisite when he laughed, and almost always of an astonishing depth and tenderness.'

Both Rimbaud boys wore trousers in a blue-grey material their mother must have bought in quantity cheaply, for their pants were the same colour during their entire school careers. They sported bowler hats and umbrellas with broken ends, because Arthur had snapped off Frédéric's umbrella-end in a door hinge and allowed him his revenge, although it meant punishment from Mother. Another time Arthur battered Delahaye's hat, knowing that in the schoolboy tit-for-tat, his own hat would be bashed, which meant a punishment of two days' bread-and-water ration at home. Delahaye saw the family as odd birds who would sometimes wear 'half-mocking smiles' – even Madame Rimbaud, 'despite her constant concern to be severe'. This smirk he called a 'family tic', noting how it hurt the feelings of those who took it for irony or lack of compassion. Sarcasm was a family trait – Arthur referred to his mother as 'la Mère Rimb', 'la *Mother*' in scornful English and the untranslatable, truculent 'la Daromphe'.

Delahaye asked endless questions of his friend, such as what he preferred to eat. Arthur said that although he was a hearty eater, he 'profoundly despised family cooking', the drab cooked vegetables and meat of the *pot-au-feu*. He preferred grilled meat 'because it's purple, with a little brown, gold, and sparklings. Also because one bites into it like a fruit.' Ernest commented, 'Love of colours was his dominating passion, and he combined it with all his desires', adding that Arthur preferred plums and 'above all' cherries, among fruits.

Most of Rimbaud's early efforts at writing are lost except for a short text written at age eight, 'Prologue', in which a traveller falls asleep under the hot sun after drinking water. Two essential subjects of his later work, sun and thirst, were already present. In 'Prologue' his parents are rich, the father choleric and mother 'gentle, calm, becoming fearful at minor things'. There is the slang exclamation 'saperlipopettouille!' which foreshadows a use of colloquial, often rude, expressions in later work. His characteristic tone and manner were there, which makes the Rimbaud phenomenon all the more terrifying to understand.

His provincial childhood was more realistically depicted in 'Poets at Age Seven', written at sixteen, which describes how, although sensitive to odours, he would lock himself in the outhouse for solitude, 'surrendering his nostrils'. He pitied shabby children whose clothes 'stank of diarrhoea' and looked at his mother with a clear blue gaze 'that lies!' He played with an eight-year-old working class girl, a 'little brute' who leapt on his back and when he was 'under her, he bit her buttocks, since she never wore underwear. Banged by her fists and heels, he brought the taste of her skin back to his room.' At seven he 'didn't love God but men', despite imposed religious study and would make up 'romances about life' lying on pieces of canvas and dreaming they were sails.

By the age of eleven Arthur was recognized as an outstanding student, but also had private interests which he listed in a notebook on ancient history: 'Darius, Cyrus, Alexander, and other accomplices remarkable for their diabolic renown.' A duality had begun between his strict home life and his imagination. As academic prizes he was given red-bound sequels to *Robinson Crusoe*, which may have inspired thoughts of distant voyages. He could be conventional, as when he sent Latin verses to Napoleon III's son to commemorate his first communion. The prince's teacher replied that he 'fully pardoned his erroneous verses' and a classmate named Jolly sniggered that he had received a 'little lesson ... for impulsively wanting to show off his know-how.'

In early adolescence he devoured books such as *Madame Bovary* and a French translation of Dickens, *Les Temps difficiles*. A friend, Paul Labarrière, lent him copies of a literary review, *Le Parnasse Contemporain*, in which he scribbled over a woman poet's line, 'I have quite heavily born my latest chagrin,' changing it to 'I have quite heavily born my latest chignon.' He loved bathroom humour, singing a ditty about a boy who won a girl's heart at a dance by claiming responsibility for a fart: 'While dancing the minuet/ at the ball/ under her skirt a little fart/ escaped on the beat. / The sensitive-nosed lover/ smelled her shame/ and at once gallantly took / responsibility for the fart./ There resulted from this fart/ a sweet marriage.'

The Charleville Collège – the equivalent of secondary school in Britain or junior high in America – offered a program of political study with half the school made up of secular students and half coming from a nearby seminary dressed in their cassocks. They banded together, reporting to the rector, a Catholic priest, about misbehaviour and liberal teachers. Arthur was seen as a double threat, being brilliantly independent and, soon, a radical. He was 'cordially detested' because he wrote assignments for secular boys, varying the style to better deceive. In one Latin composition class a student wearing a cassock told the teacher, 'Sir, Rimbaud is cheating. He's passing a note to his neighbour.' Arthur rose up halfway from his chair, tossed his Latin thesaurus at the head of the complainer, and then 'sat back down, stoic and disdainful'.

At thirteen he told Delahaye that the arch-conservative Napoleon III deserved to be punished as a galley slave. Either his opinions had changed since the royal congratulatory verses or they had been a pose to begin with. Delahaye was 'terrified and enchanted' at such opinions: 'How interesting life had become!' The boys discussed gruesome details of history such as the Spanish Inquisition and the martyrdom of Jan Hus. Even before having reading Sade, Rimbaud sought out sadistic moments in history. When he was fourteen he wrote prize-winning Latin assignments that were published in a local educational bulletin: 'The Angel and the Child' translated into Latin a sentimental French poem about a boy threatened by a supernatural being to which he added an original scene of a dead child appearing to his mother. Another poem translated from Horace, 'The Schoolboy's Dream', told of doves carrying a boy away to crown him a poet after he was 'tired from playing', but Arthur significantly described him as lying down when his 'limbs were broken' by 'long vagabondage'.

Volunteering for another competition, he digressed from the theme to explain his decision to become a writer. His message was that France's past national glory inspired him to be a hero, but current humiliations stymied colonial dreams and forced a 'retreat' to literature. In Arthur's life this retreat would prove only temporary, as France suffered the humiliations of the 1870 war, including invasion and a humiliating defeat at the hands of the Prussians, and the subsequent Commune, when Socialist Frenchmen tried to take their country's destiny into their own hands, only to fail tragically. Even before these developments, young Arthur was already writing about a France in decline from former majesties:

If we again recall ancient times when we owned an abundance of all sorts of property and when our colonial cities spread across the whole world, when we subjugated all Asia and almost all Italy, what else can we feel but regret to recall our past glory and prosperity, what else but rage and pain when we think of the destiny that awaits our Gaul. Since the ineluctable law of the gods has decided that she will now be defeated and despised as was Greece, that mother and nurse of warriors, let us banish entirely the idea of glory from our memories. We are left with the consolation of belles-lettres, the study of thought, a joy that remains amid pain, and a sort of shadow of freedom amid servitude. No more on public affairs, which can no longer concern us, but on poetry, the immortal gods, all the objects which (Homer and Plato) spoke so well about.

After three or four years of thus embracing literature, he reclaimed the former ambition to be a colonial adventurer when France had recovered. Despite his genius, literature was consciously an intense interlude, not a permanent self-definition, so he was able to take all the risks and achieve what he did during the short time in which he wrote. From this early age, then, his life's plan was largely set: the question was how to implement what he already saw as his particular destiny. Part of it was literary, part of it sexual. If literature was a temporary choice, his sexual identity was not. It is unlikely that early gay feelings would have isolated him at school; recollections by others state that homosexuality was common at the Charleville Collège or as one witness put it, 'inversion was rather frequent, as in all schools'. A local educator drew up a plan to omit pockets from school uniforms because students were slitting them open to masturbate, hands in pockets, during class: 'Sometimes students even masturbate under the very eyes of the teacher who surveys them. The danger is especially great when the teacher turns his back on students and cannot even observe on their faces the muscular convulsions which reveal the moment of ejaculation.' If Arthur participated in this trend, he did not share the fate of another writer, André Gide, who was expelled from a Paris school for masturbating too often in class.

On the contrary, he was outwardly obedient but obsessed with the empowerment of adolescence. He scrawled caricatures of old men in a copybook, captioning them 'senile, senile, senile …' He sought allies in his struggle to realize his already ripe potential; one such was the eighteenth-century French philosopher Claude-Adrien Helvétius, author of 'De l'Homme', who argued that adolescents were superior to adults, stating, 'At the spring of life, like the spring of the year, sap climbs powerfully in trees. In youth a man's sublime thoughts form inside him which must one day make him famous.' To help realize his dreams of achievement, Arthur also found a sympathetic teacher, a twenty-two year old liberal, Georges Izambard, new to teaching and intrigued by his intelligence. While perhaps not going so far as Helvétius in claiming adolescents' superiority, Izambard was for a time willing to lend a patient, amused ear to his student's urgent declarations. Izambard later scoffed when he was called 'Rimbaud's teacher' since he had been dominated by the boy's mental power just as future generations of readers would be dominated by his achievements. Izambard sympathized for a while with Arthur's intellectual ambitions but despite one later writer's suggestion, he did not spark 'homo-erotic desires' in the boy. But the gawky teacher provided liberation by lending books. Madame Rimbaud hated literature and set herself as censor. Arthur loved no person as much as he loved books, and getting between him and his love was dangerous. One writer has stated, 'Poets of Rimbaud's nature do not have time to read books in the meticulous way that scholars do,' but at the Charleville library Arthur studied old treatises on witchcraft, eighteenth-century opera librettos, libertine novels, contemporary French poetry, including Hugo and Musset whom he disliked, Théophile Gautier, Leconte de Lisle, Théodore de Banville, Albert Mérat, and Paul Verlaine, whom he admired. He had begun to write original poems, his earliest surviving effort being the sentimental 'Orphans' New Year's Present' which mourned a dead mother in a way that may have been wishful thinking. He strove for publication, sending it to *la Revue pour tous*, which advised him to cut it by a third, which he did; it was published on January 2, 1870. He sent verses and stories to newspaper editors and wrote to noted poets to advance his literary career. His early poems are often long and bellicose. 'The Blacksmith' was a monologue fit for the likes of the actor Gérard Depardieu, in which a revolutionary leader harangued King Louis XVI at the Tuileries Palace in 1792. 'We are scum,' announced the revolutionary to the 'old bedizened kings ... shit on these dogs!' The narrator noted, 'We kissed our sons against our chests', a scene of a revolutionary-era eroticism.

Another long poem, 'Sun and Flesh', was about man's decline from a mythic golden age of 'lascivious satyrs, animal fauns'. Eroticized gods included a 'white Callypygia and little Cupid'. Buttocks would be important in Rimbaud's later imagery and it is significant that he had already cited the Greek goddess of beautiful backsides, Callypygia. In early 1870 Izambard assigned his class a composition, 'A Letter from the Poet Charles d'Orléans to King Louis XI asking for a pardon for the criminal poet François Villon,' in jail under sentence of death. For documentation Izambard lent him Villon's poems, Théodore de Banville's play, *Gringoire* and Hugo's *Notre-Dame de Paris*, but Madame Rimbaud wrote complaining that *Les Misérables* by 'Victor Hugot is a dangerous model.' Izambard assured her that he had not given the boy *Les Misérables*, which contained the word 'shit' in a chapter on Waterloo. He did give Arthur a key to his study, where the student exhausted the library and used it as a safe house for his own reading materials. There Arthur would enjoy books 'like a rat in his cheese' but Izambard never heard any gratitude since his pupil 'didn't know how to say thank you. Where could he have learned it from?'

In his 'Letter from the poet Charles d'Orléans', Arthur stated that Villon gave up bourgeois comfort and frequented prostitutes and taverns because of his identity as poet. Criminality and sexual license gave him the 'diabolic renown' he relished. Arthur recognized poets as a race apart and in his letter had Charles d'Orléans tell the King that poets 'are not from down here: let them live their strange life, be cold and hungry, run, love, and sing ... all these mad children, for their souls are full of rhymes that laugh and weep, that make us laugh or weep: Let them live: God blesses all misericordia, and the world blesses poets.' Arthur knew that Villon was reportedly hanged for his crimes, and may have known about his reputed homosexuality. He embraced the identity of the doomed or damned poet (*poète maudit*), happy to fulfil his mother's fears and suffer the worst punishment.

All the while, in class Arthur was 'hermetic and reticent', but in private conversations he 'bloomed like a King of intellectual gaiety', Izambard later stated. He added that the boy never 'took advantage' of their friendship, meaning that he asked for no academic favours and perhaps never discussed inappropriate subjects such as homosexuality. Decades later when an interviewer asked Izambard what role homosexuality played in Arthur's 'disordering of all the senses', he cut off the question, saying, 'You know very well that at the time nobody talked about that yet.' In 1930 Izambard would write to a homophobic biographer named Godchot that once he would have shared his 'violent disgust' about homosexuality and agreed with 'your diatribes, your anathema', but for him the time for disgust was 'no more. It isn't because I've been visited belatedly by the passions of Count Charlus. I haven't got such aristocratic tastes.' But forty years earlier, around 1890, he had had 'a revision of values. I recognized that in the domain of follies called love and sensuality, we haven't the right, myself or anyone else, to set ourselves up as judges of our fellow men.'

Arthur's first poems abided by heterosexual conventions: in 'To Music', about a military band playing in front of the Charleville railway station, bloated and ugly locals gathered while the poet stared with violent desire at schoolgirls. Yet girls were dismissed in 'Novel', written at the same time, because they laugh at the young poet's sonnets. The poem, containing the ironic line 'One isn't serious at seventeen' was divided into four 'chapters' as a novel of non-fulfilment, and the narrator took to drink after his disappointment. As described in 'To Music' an explosion seemed imminent since the poet could no longer bear the town or its people. For the time being, Arthur wrote with publication in mind and some early works reflect literary formulas of the day. 'Sleeper in the Valley' became one of his best-known poems. He used a favourite word, 'hole', to set the scene: 'it's a verdant hole' where the soldier lies. The fact that the soldier is dead is predictable, and Arthur, who could focus pitilessly on physical decay, was uncharacteristically decorous in limiting the signs of death to two neat bullet holes. The dead soldier was a romantic object in the tradition of the martyred ephebe in French history painting exemplified in David's *Death of Bara*, in which a nude boy is stretched out in pathetic glory.

On May 24, 1870 Rimbaud wrote to the poet Théodore de Banville, the leader of a literary group called the Parnassians, hoping to be published in *Le Parnasse contemporain*. The seductive letter began 'Dear Master, We are in the months of love, and I'm seventeen.' Arthur was only fifteen but wished to be at 'the age of hopes and chimera'. His poems were not published by Banville who nonetheless saved them. But Rimbaud continued as the dynamic force, the hunter, and, as Delahaye put it, 'the little conscript had a veteran's authority, to which were joined the seduction of vivacities, acidities, and childish candours.' Three months after Arthur's letter to Banville, on July 19, France declared war on Prussia, and a month later, *La Charge* published his 'Three Kisses'. He wrote a number of other poems, including 'Venus Anadyomene' and 'Nina's Replies'. The grotesque tradition of Northern art was evident in 'Venus Anadyomene', describing a grossly fat woman, 'her wide crotch hideously embellished with an anal ulcer.' 'Nina's Replies' also deflated heterosexual romance with details of peasant life: 'It will smell of the stable, full of warm dungheaps ... a cow will dung proudly at every step.'

On August 29, 1870, after the school year was over and Arthur had won a number of academic prizes, he ran away from home for the first time to nearby Charleroi where he spent the day of the 30th. His brother Frédéric had previously run away to join the army, and this may have impelled his decision. The next day he arrived at Paris' Gare du Nord without a ticket or identification papers. He was arrested and taken to the Mazas prison for a few days until he divulged his name and address. On September 2 Napoleon III surrendered to the Prussians and two days later the Third Republic was proclaimed. The next day Arthur wrote to his teacher asking for help and was freed into his custody, staying at the home of Izambard's adoptive aunts in the northern city of Douai. There Arthur copied out a number of his poems to be given to a young poet Izambard knew, Paul Demeny. On September 26 Arthur took the train back to Charleville with Izambard and his classmate, Léon Deverrière, but by October 2 he had run away again, to Brussels, and did not return until a month later. Once again he took refuge at the home of Izambard's aunts in Douai until his mother called the police to get him home.

Poems from this time, 'At the Cabaret Vert' and 'The Sly Women', expressed pleasure at sitting and eating after tramping around all day. The waitress in both poems was more maternal than sexual, with her 'huge tits' an invitation to nurse. A short poem, 'My Bohemia', transformed experience into metaphor as Arthur walked, fists in his torn pockets, and his 'coat also turned into the ideal'. He promised to be a vassal of the Muse, wearing his only pair of pants with a large hole in them. In 'The Seated Ones', an unhelpful Charleville librarian whose eyes 'seep black poison' left him 'trapped in an atrocious funnel'. The poem has the incantatory power of an Irish curse. In contrast to these words-as-weapons, 'Customs Officials' is funny, especially its last six lines describing the officers' pomposity and mundane chatter: 'They grab Fausts and Fra Diavolos/ 'None of that, old boys! Put down those bundles.' Delahaye stated that the poem was about a trip he and Arthur made to Belgium to smuggle tobacco during the 1870 war. The poem's last line, 'It's hell for the offenders who have been frisked by his palm', referred to a body search at the French border.

From late October 1870, Arthur's behaviour became outwardly provocative. Instead of his previous neat appearance, he wore his hair long in what he called a Merovingian style. He would steal books from local stores and replace them when finished – until he decided to sell them to avoid being caught bringing them back. His language, once polite unless he was upset by his mother, became rude and he wrote scatalogical poems. 'Evening Prayer' is a mock-exalted description of a beer drinker who gets through 'thirty or forty tankards' and then goes outside to 'piss toward the brown heavens'. Dreams burning inside the drinker are like 'hot excrements in an old dove-cote'. Another poem, 'Squattings', depicted a priest shitting into a chamberpot and 'Parisian War Song' used scatology to convey delirious involvement with the Commune: 'O May! What delirious naked arses!' Both poems used the word 'sniffings', and 'sniffer' ('renifleur') was a nineteenth-century slang for a gay man who hung around urinals in search of sex. In the political satire, 'The Smashing Victory at Sarrebrück', a soldier presented his buttocks to the viewer as a symbol of the way French country people were exploited by the Emperor. 'My Beloved Little Girls' is a poem of vehement misoygny and invective in which every woman is an 'ugly one'. Despite the violence of the line, 'I'd like to break your hips for having loved,' Arthur apparently never struck a woman in his life.

'Lice Pickers' was a transfigured genre scene, a favourite of early translators of the poet while 'First Communions' was a heavy-breathing allegory about the effect of the 'putrid kiss of Jesus' upon women. Theorizing about women's needs and church-going was a response to Michelet's rhapsodic 'Woman', but the poem is too theoretical for its own good, and another bookish tirade against religion, 'The Just Man', survived in a fragment. The poem 'Sisters of Charity' is generally taken to be a misogynistic statement, yet more important is the narcissistic self-portrait of a 'young man whose eyes are brilliant, skin brown, and lovely twenty-year-old body which should go naked and, forehead ringed in copper, be worshipped under the moon in Persia by an unknown Genius.' His attempts to contact renowned writers were part of a quest for a worshipper-genius to achieve 'immense dreams or walks across nights of truth'. The reference to Persia may be an identification with the pederastic tradition in old Middle Eastern poetry and the word genius, in French génie, conjures up the *Arabian Nights*.

A comical prose piece from this time, 'A Heart Beneath a Cassock', was not published until 1924 when French Surrealists took it as a prototype, although it is really no more surrealist than the Grossmith brothers' *Diary of a Nobody*. It tells of a clergy student with stinking feet who writes an absurd love poem. So great is the sexual repression in his school that he is reprimanded for spreading his legs in study hall, 'more and more notoriously each day, like a slovenly young man.' The repression explodes in an unconsciously obscene ode to his beloved. 'In its cotton retreat, the sweet-breathed zephyr sleeps ... with a jolly chin!' The zephyr, or penis, lifts its wing in erection, and 'smells real good'. Listeners to the ode include a Madame

Riflandouille whose name means 'to pare sausages made of chitter-lings', another phallic reference. The prose is notable for its deadpan, stoic-comedian quality and despite slapstick interludes there is a shapely form to the story, including the final announcement that the boy will become a priest and continue to wear the same socks until he reaches Paradise. Toned down, 'A Heart Beneath a Cassock' might have been published as a merry spoof and perhaps launched a successful career in comic prose. Instead, with school closed because of the war, Arthur was limited to reading and taking walks with Delahaye. He sent poems and articles to a local newspaper founded in November, le Progrès des Ardennes, but literary ambitions were distracted when the nearby city of Mézières was shelled by the Germans on December 31 and on January 1, 1871 Charleville and Mézières were occupied.

France was defeated; peace treaties were signed on January 28 and on February 17, and the veteran politician Thiers became leader of France. Eight days later, Arthur was on a train to Paris in time to see German troops marching down the Champs-Elysées. He had no money and no friends so he slept in the open air with clochards on the Left Bank before returning to Charleville on foot by March 10. On March 18 the Commune was established, a socialist movement in reaction to the social iniquities of the regime. The Communards suffered famine, mass execution and exile in war-torn and blockaded Paris. Arthur supported the Commune in poems such as 'Parisian War Song', 'Jeanne-Marie's Hands', and 'Parisian Orgy, or the city is Repopulated'. 'Jeanne-Marie's Hands' praised a woman as a killing machine: her hands 'will twist your necks, O evil women and crush your hands, noblewomen.' 'Parisian Orgy' was a vast historical canvas pointing to the paradox that although the city is 'a stinking ulcer over green nature', its beauty is 'splendid'. The Commune was part of the consecration of the city as 'supreme poetry'. Despite conflicting testimonies, Arthur was probably not in Paris during the Commune. Letters prove that he was in Charleville on April 17 and May 13, and without money he would have had to walk to Paris, a week away. On May 13 he wrote a long letter of poetic theory to Izambard, whereas, had he just made the trip, he would have been travel-worn. More likely he cheered the Communards from Charleville. The French monarchy installed at Versailles bombarded Paris's suburbs at the beginning of May and invaded the city on May 21, beginning what was known as the Bloody Week.

Parts of Arthur's May 13 letter to Izambard have become as famous as some of his poems. He wrote that he was busy 'wallowing in vice' with the goal of being a poet and 'seer': 'It's a matter of arriving at the unknown by the disordering of all the senses. The sufferings are enormous, but one must be strong, be born a poet, and I have recognized myself as a poet.' The phrase ' "*Je*" *est un autre*', (' "I" ' is another person') refers to a kind of subjective poetry he was rejecting for a more objective or distanced writing. He told Izambard, 'You are not a teacher for me' and offered a poem, asking him not to underline it with pencil as if grading an exam or even read it with too much thought. The poem was 'The Tortured Heart', which begins 'My sad heart drools at the stern'.

'The Tortured Heart' expressed defilement in the face of military sexuality ('*ithyphallique et pioupiesque*' literally, erect penis and army-like, referring to the French Emperor's forces at Versailles, known as *pioupious*). In 'The Tortured Heart' laughter is animalistic mocking of the sacred heart of Jesus; 'take my heart, that it may be washed' is a plea for baptismal cleansing. Yet the 'gushings' ('*flots*') in which the cleansing will take place is a word also applied to ejaculation. Utterly serious, describing violent clowning and implying sex and religion, the poem has too many dimensions to be translated in a single way. Its power comes in part from a strict traditional form, the *triolet*, strong dancing rhythms, and surprising rhymes. In this poem, like many by Rimbaud, the reader cannot be sure of what is going on, but is convinced of the majesty of the writer's inspiration.

It is a leap of the imagination to assume that the poet described a scene in which he was raped, yet the poem has routinely been read this way. One French biographer, Robert Arnoult, published a version of the supposed rape with dialogue invented for the Communards: 'Okay, kid, now strip!' A more recent biographer described the supposed rape scene where soldiers 'jeer as he is buggered'. However, it is unlikely that Arthur was raped by Communards since he continued to support them, writing poems sympathetic to their aims and in London and Brussels visited exiles of the movement. If rape there was, it more likely occurred when Arthur was imprisoned at Mazas in 1870 for riding a train to Paris without a ticket. Izambard remembered that when Arthur arrived in Paris two policemen 'body-searched him' (*'fouillé à fond'*), which may have been enough of a violation to inspire the poem. The myth of a Communard rape was motivated not just by anti-Commune propaganda but also by homophobia. Some critics claim that after being raped by Communards Arthur made a brief but conscious choice to 'experiment' with homosexuality, which he then quickly regretted. For these writers the poet's gay life, entirely negative, logically began with a rape.

Izambard also misread 'Tortured Heart', although in a different way, thinking it satiric nonsense – Arthur was partly to blame for suggesting that this was how his teacher would read the poem – and answered with a dull parody of the poem. This ended the friendship, but the letter in which Arthur had sent the poem had already begun to cast Izambard off. He had no need of an instructor on his voyage to the heart of poetry where he accepted suffering as experience: Delahaye told how the two friends were crossing a dense forest outside Charleville and Arthur accidentally scraped his head on the thorny trunk of a young robinia tree. Delahaye said, 'You're bleeding,' to which Arthur replied, 'It's the thorn of thought.'

On May 15, two days after his letter to Izambard with 'The Tortured Heart', he sent Demeny another letter of intent, known as 'the seer letter', with three new poems, 'Parisian War Song', 'My Little Beloved Girls', and 'Crouchings'. Three weeks later he sent another letter to Demeny with more poems, 'Poets at Age Seven', 'Poor People at Church', and 'The Tortured Heart'. He stated that the poet becomes a seer by a willed 'disordering of all the senses'. Critics who believe that his homosexuality was consciously planned and not innate, cite this text, although gay sex was not a 'sense' in the way he meant it. Odour, for example, was. In 'The Poor at Church', a contrast is made between Jesus, who is 'far from the smells of meat and moldy fabric', and the church itself, 'warmed stinkingly by the breath' of poor worshippers who are 'sniffing the smell of wax like the aroma of bread'. As grotesques, the poor were 'drooling a beggarly, stupid faith'. To drivel (*baver*) was one of Arthur's favourite verbs, used in 'My Little Beloved Girls' and in 'The Tortured Heart'.

Trying to change all his perceptions for the sake of art, Arthur was not satisfied with his own disorderings but sought new ways of seeing, hearing, smelling, tasting, and otherwise perceiving experience. How these disorderings were to take place is a matter still discussed by Rimbaud's readers. Responses have ranged from free sexual expression, drugs, alcohol, and other activities indisputably part of the poet's life. His willingness to sleep rough, accepting body lice and personal uncleanliness, were part of his refusal to take anything for granted, even the minimum of comfort. Still, it does not suffice to be an alcoholic drug-abusing homeless gay man to write poems as great as

Rimbaud's. The still-mysterious missing ingredients have meant that France has not seen a poet of his power for over a hundred years.

Aware of his uniqueness, Arthur still sought fellowship in his quest. He urged other poets to follow suit, although his exhortations usually fell on deaf ears. He signed a second letter to Banville, dated August 15, 'Achille Bava', or 'Achilles Drooled', enclosing a poem, 'What the Poet is Told About Flowers'. He addressed Banville as a poet of the future, calling for 'what is new = ideas and forms'. Lilies were called 'those enemas of ecstasy' and the flower Açoka was mentioned to play on the words 'Açoka cadre', which sounds like 'caca', the infantile word for shit. He asked if a flower, 'dead or alive, is worth one shit from a seabird' and urged Banville on to wilder discoveries, to find flowers that are chairs or 'almost stones' in a fabulous new natural history. Banville remained firmly entrenched in his traditionalist approach to literature, and is today almost completely forgotten as a writer, despite some early satirically tinged works with some measure of interest.

At this time Arthur wrote 'The Drunken Boat', following two lesser efforts, 'First Communions' and 'The Just Man'. Instead of bemoaning church hypocrisies, he charted his own imaginative voyages, fuelled by voracious reading which probably included Poe's *Adventures of Arthur Gordon Pym*, Verne's *20,000 Leagues Under the Sea*, and Hugo's *Travailleurs de la Mer*. He had never actually seen the sea but had sailed toy boats on the Meuse River in Charleville. A mood of savagery was established in the opening lines, with the author no longer guided by haulers: 'Gaudy redskins used them as targets, having nailed them naked to coloured stakes.' While past poems often focused on odours, 'Drunken Boat' was a highly visual experience: wines are blue and the sky green. The bitter redness of love fermented the 'bluenesses' and the sun lit up 'long purple coagulations'. The traveller dreamed of a 'green night with dazzled snows' and the 'blue-yellow awakening of phosphorus singers'. Drenched in this colour-field abstraction, the subject was of secondary concern. Such poetic force in unforgettable lines could only have been achieved by a great writer. He was sixteen.

At around this time he became acquainted with Charles Auguste Bretagne, an office employee in Charleville who enjoyed sitting in taverns, smoking a pipe and quaffing beer. By speaking to those who knew Bretagne, the biographer Marcel Coulon discovered that the anti-clerical, left-wing bachelor, then in his early thirties, was gay. Whether or not Bretagne had a sexual relationship with Arthur is unknown, but he bought beer, wine and tobacco for the boy and relished his imaginatively obscene talk. Bretagne, a jolly rotund man, lived for a time at the same boarding house as Izambard, which was probably how he got to know Arthur, and by chance he was also a friend of Paul Verlaine. A caricature by Paul depicted the walrus-like Bretagne carrying a huge *baguette* under his arm like a giant condom. It was Bretagne who, after letters to other poets had no effect, suggested that Arthur write to Paul: 'Mention my name. Maybe he can do something for you.' Taking Bretagne's advice, Arthur sent a letter to Verlaine, followed almost immediately by a second, containing his poems 'The Transfixed Ones', 'Crouchings', 'Custom Officials', 'The Tortured Heart', 'The Seated Ones', 'My Little Beloved Girls', 'First Communions', and 'Paris Repopulates'. He didn't send 'Drunken Boat', saving it for later as a surprise. Phrases only survive from the two men's letters. Paul replied, 'You are prodigiously armed ... Come, great soul, we are calling you, we are waiting for you.' (The '*on*' in '*on t'appelle*' is often used as a polite way to refer to oneself, so the sentence may also be translated as 'I am calling you, I am waiting for you.') The most famous gay couple in modern literary history would soon be united.

RIMBAUD, AS CARICATURED BY VERLAINE

With Verlaine: 1871–1872

Paul Verlaine (1844–1896) was one of the outstanding French lyric poets of his century. With an unusual musical sensitivity to the sound of the language, he wrote fresh and free lyrics, that have attracted composers for song settings. Born in Metz, he soon came to Paris, where he lived with his mother and worked in offices, first in an insurance company and then as a clerk at the Paris Hôtel de Ville. He published poems in *Le Parnasse Contemporain* and produced in 1867 a collection of libertine lyrics, *The Women Friends* (*Les Amies*), which was banned by a French court the following year. At the same time he began to attend the socially important Paris arts salon of the hostess Nina de Villard. In 1869 his collection *Fêtes Galantes* appeared, and the following year *La Bonne Chanson* celebrated his love for his adolescent bride Mathilde Mauté. Both books had a lightness and natural grace that hearkened back to the eighteenth century, qualities that would later attract Rimbaud, perhaps for its difference from their own artistic qualities and goals.

Despite his wide acceptance in the nineteenth-century French arts world, Verlaine was one of the more socially helpless poets of his or any generation. Continually dependent on others for money, food, drink, and lodgings, he was all too often reduced to piteous states, which he would usually endure with some measure of humour, calling himself 'Pauvre Lélian', or 'Poor Lélian', an anagram of his name. Less amusingly, Verlaine would lash out at his benefactors, particularly at women close to him. His conduct exceeded the patience of many observers: the biographer Godchot snapped, 'Poor Lélian, *Pouah!*'

Among his other vagaries, Paul was an alcoholic who indulged in absinthe, the green drink notorious for causing nerve damage. Linked to his alcoholism were his outbursts of domestic violence against his mother, his wife, and on one occasion, his baby son. Pathology ran in the family: Paul's mother kept three of her miscarried fetuses in fluid-filled jars locked in a bedroom cabinet. During one of his fits Paul broke open the cabinet and dashed the jars to the ground whereupon his mother buried the fetuses in the backyard.

He was also bisexual, although ultimately preferring men: as a youngster he fell in love with a male cousin, Dujardin, speaking of him, according to one friend, 'like a lover praising his mistress'. A classmate at the lycée Bonaparte, Lucien Viotti, was another lover lauded in Paul's 'Memoirs of a Widower' for the 'exquisite proportions of your ephebe's body in the costume of a gentleman.' After Arthur there would be a series of male lovers, including, according to some writers, Germain Nouveau and Lucien Létinois, a farm lad whom he unofficially adopted and whose death sparked 'a violent frenzy of homosexual sensuality'. His sexual complexities have been a minefield for critics: the 1920s biographer Marcel Coulon stated that Verlaine chose to be gay because he was too ugly to attract women and was 'one of those who are not able to wait. A great number of homosexuals are people who could not wait. For lack of thrushes, they satisfy themseves with blackbirds, which are taken more easily because they too often cannot wait'. Even recently, the biographer Joanna Richardson suggested that Verlaine's homosexuality 'owed something to his ugliness', although her book appeared at a time when 'ugly' or 'impatient' were no longer generally acceptable synonyms for 'gay'.

Paul had a feline side, called 'feminine' by critics who used the word in the Victorian context of woman-as-victim. His *Confessions of a Poet* describes a childhood illness when a leech was applied as treatment and when his mother returned she found his 'small bed red with blood, and I myself had swooned'. The bleeding is recounted with menstrual pride, a sanguinary excitement that would continue in his consensual S-M relationship with Arthur.

Biographers may have been misled in their diagnoses of Paul's behaviour by the poet's own often-confused estimations of his character and desires. In 1870 he married a quiet bourgeois seventeen-year-old, Mathilde Mauté, who was fourteen when she met him and sixteen when they became engaged. He saw marriage as a way of curbing his alcoholism and perhaps his gay sex life. But in fact he always joked about his gayness with friends and would write homoerotic verse which he circulated widely, only denying he was gay to those who might be offended by the fact. One such, Mathilde's father, a stuffy old party, added the noble but fictitious suffix 'de Fleurville' to the family name. Paul detested him and wrote a couplet, 'To kill a father-in-law, one must decide/ to immortalize oneself through a fine parricide,' punning on 'beau-père' (father-in-law) and 'beau parricide'. Her mother was a refined hostess and music teacher whose pupils included the young Claude Debussy, and her half-brother Charles de Sivry, who lived with them, composed witty operettas. By entering this family Paul greatly enriched his cultural ties, yet he was soon bored at the idea of marriage, to a woman at least. During their courtship he wrote a series of love lyrics, *La Bonne Chanson*, of which some were later set to music by Fauré. Although inspired by his love, he felt the typical bisexual's dilemma of not being entirely fulfilled by a woman. More importantly, he saw sex as a giddy exploration of what he called one of the fine arts, '*luxure*', or lewdness. With this empirical attitude of life as a sexual laboratory, it was natural that sparks would fly when he met the teenaged Arthur, out to disorder all his senses.

When he replied to Arthur's letters he thought him a twenty-ish provincial poet. Their first meeting had the shock of discovery. Verlaine and a poet friend, Charles Cros, had dawdled at the railway station bar and missed him, which suggests that Paul was not expecting this to be the decisive emotional encounter of his life. Arthur found his own way to the Mauté home where Mathilde and her mother received him. Paul soon arrived and he later published recollections of his first sight of Arthur: 'The real head of a child, chubby and fresh, on a big, bony rather clumsy body of a still-growing adolescent, and whose voice, with a very strong Ardennes accent that was almost a dialect, had highs and lows as if it were breaking.' Paul would mock Arthur's pronounciations: *dargnières* instead of *dernières* (latest), and *junesse* instead of *jeunesse* (youth). He did not mention the menacing look Arthur could have, but Mathilde did: 'His eyes were blue, rather handsome, but they had the sullen expression that in our indulgence we took for timidity.'

Arthur's expression could also be interpreted as perverse. A friend of Paul's, Léon Valade, described him thus in October 1871: 'Big hands and feet, an absolutely childish face that could have belonged to a boy of thirteen, deep blue eyes, character more savage than shy, that's the kid whose imagination full of power and unbelievable corruption has fascinated and terrified all our friends.' Arthur had sprouted up in height recently from 1.6m (5ft 3in) in January 1871 to 1.73m (5ft 8in) at the end of the year. Soon he would reach his full height of about 1.77m or 1.8m (5ft 10in–6ft). His long legs were strongly muscled by his endless rambles, 'matchless legs' as Paul would call them. Paul at twenty-six was, according to Delahaye, 'timid and supple, with a delicate, sweet and ardent face.' His flat nose and slanted Mongol eyes, patchy beard, oddly shaped head and long neck were fodder for caricaturists, including himself: he scribbled self-portraits as a pigtailed Chinaman.

The exact beginning of their sexual relationship is uncertain, but the most plausible scholarly arguments place it sooner rather than later after their meeting. Paul's manifest delight at Arthur's misbehaviour in the Mauté home, their frequent absences together, and other signs point to an immediate complicity of the closest kind. Arthur was a difficult houseguest, asking Mathilde to take down from the wall of his room a portrait of a distant Mauté relative because it had mold on the forehead and this 'upset and worried' him. He stole a favourite ivory crucifix of hers, walking with it through the Latin Quarter 'brasseries of whores'. Long before widespread concern for animal rights, friends were shocked when he blew hot ash from his pipe into the nostril of a carriage horse in the street. A typical country upbringing had taught him casual cruelty to animals, yet Petitfils oddly attributed such mistreatments to 'a certain impetuosity of character rather than to cruelty.' These infractions enchanted Paul who took vicarious pleasure in his unconcern with bourgeois propriety.

Paul did everything possible to see that his literary friends recognized Arthur's talent, and for the most part they did. He took Arthur to the photographer Etienne Carjat, and at a meeting of writer friends called the *Vilains bonshommes* ('the Naughty Chaps') Rimbaud read his 'Drunken Boat' to positive reactions and Banville, as guest of honour, had no objection except that it seemed 'odd' to make a boat speak. Arthur did not reply but on his way out shrugged his shoulders and grumbled, 'Old idiot' (*'vieux con'*). Probably in early 1872 he wrote the sonnet 'Vowels' which attributed different colours to vowel sounds. Academia loves such systems and this poem has been studied to death, but as Paul told the poet Pierre Louÿs, Arthur 'didn't give a fuck if 'A' was red or green, he just saw things that way, that's all.'

A more personal poem was 'Young Couple', dated June 27, 1872 , a portrait of Paul's marriage. Outside the walls of a young couple's room

'COIN DE TABLE' PAINTED BY FANTIN-LATOUR
VERLAINE AND RIMBAUD ARE SEATED AT THE LEFT OF THE TABLE

the 'gums of imps vibrate', in a lewd evocation of fellatio disturbing marital calm. One of Paul's friends, Edmond Lepelletier, a bourgeois man of letters, never admitted in print that V&R were lovers, but in private he knew since he received letters from Paul full of gay jokes. Pierre Loüys' *Journal* for July 1890 records Lepelletier's boast to friends 'that he had never been fucked in the ass by Verlaine'. Lepelletier called Arthur 'neurotic and hysteric', claiming his influence on Paul was personally disastrous and artistically insignificant. At Paul's insistence, Lepelletier invited Arthur to dinner, where the boy was sullen and violent, and made menacing gestures with a dessert knife. His host warned him that he'd fought in the Franco-Prussian War and was not afraid of Prussians or 'street urchins'. Arthur's retreat behind a cloud of pipe smoke suggested that his behaviour was really play-acting.

In a theatre review of November 15, 1871, Lepelletier wrote that Paul was seen at a play's première with 'a Mademoiselle Rimbaut on his arm'. The same article also described the writer Catulle Mendès, known to be heterosexual, on the arm of a male friend. Walking arm-in-arm was socially acceptable but Lepelletier made the 'Mademoiselle' joke because in fact V&R had walked with their arms around each others' necks. The journalist was acting as social censor, just as an unsigned item, perhaps also by Lepelletier, printed in the daily *XIXième siècle* on November 17 described Paul's attacks on his wife without naming him. Other observers would also liken young Arthur to a girl, as the younger partner in a known pederastic couple: Stéphane Mallarmé wrote that Arthur, whom he met at a dinner of the Naughty Chaps, 'had something proudly, or nastily, forward like a girl of the people of the laundress variety, due to vast hands red with chillblains due to the transition from hot to cold. Which would have indicated worse jobs, belonging to a boy.' And Rémy de Gourmont described Arthur in an 1891 article as 'one of those women about whom one isn't surprised to hear it said that she converted to religion in a whorehouse. But what is even more revolting is that he seems to have been a jealous and passionate mistress: here aberration becomes crapulous, being sentimental.' Playing with his gender was not an innocent game to those who typed him as a catamite. Yet Mallarmé admired Arthur in his *Divagations* as a 'considerable passerby, operating alive on poetry,' while Gourmont grudgingly admitted in *The Book of Masks* that he was 'somebody, in spite of everything'.

Arthur left the Mauté home before he was asked to go and lodged for a time with Charles Cros, a poet and inventor who created the first prototype for the phonograph. Cros was a target of Arthur's pranks – he cut his poems out of literary reviews and used them as toilet paper, and chipped the nose off a marble statue, yet Cros was saddened when V&R left Paris, for he was fascinated by Arthur's talent and amused by the couple. After Cros could no longer house Arthur, he stayed for a time with Ernest Cabaner, a composer and pianist who was known to be gay and may have briefly been his lover. Cabaner lived in a hovel which Arthur made even less habitable by cutting holes in a glass pane to let in the winter air. The place was strewn with filthy old shoes he used as flowerpots.

Cabaner's etiolated features were likened by Paul to 'Jesus Christ after three years of absinthe' and he wrote a parody song about him based on a popular ditty of the time, 'The Bearded Lady'. He also drew a caricature of Cabaner, standing near a piano, sucking his own penis. A verse by Valade written above it asks, 'Has the divine Cabaner/ eaten his sons, like Saturn?' In an age of rude parlour tricksters such as Le Pétomane, a vaudevillian who farted musically, perhaps the scrawny Cabaner was enough of a contortionist to be an auto-fellator. This renown for sperm ingestion would explain an anecdote preserved by Delahaye in which Arthur claimed to have masturbated into a glass of milk poured by Cabaner, who unwittingly drank it. Whatever his other abilities, Cabaner did write a poem to welcome Arthur on his arrival in Paris after Paul's friends chipped in to pay for the train ticket. It appeared in the Zutiste Album (discussed below), starting as an ironic monologue by Madame Rimbaud, known to the friends only as a pious and stingy provincial widow: 'Criminals against your youth/ Some friends, having read your verse/ together have paid your voyage/ accomplices of your perverse plan/ May they be damned in the name of your Mother/ these impudent Parnassians!' The poem changed to the voice of a potential male lover, either Paul or Cabaner: 'It was to test the depths of your nature, / child, that I spoke this way/ But I offer you: food,/ clothing ... bed, if you want: / Yes, I'll be more than a mother/ to you, since for a long while/ Looking for a

friend on this earth/ I'm waiting, I'm waiting, I'm waiting.' In reply
Arthur wrote 'Remembrances of the Idiotic Old Fellow' on the
following page of the album, a sexual free-for-all in which a man
expressed desire for his mother, father, and sister, ending with the cry,
'Let's jerk off!'

Meanwhile the Verlaine marriage was on the rocks. Mathilde gave
birth to a boy, Georges, on October 30, 1871 and less than a week
later Paul made violent scenes while Mathilde withdrew into a silent
shell of depression, reacting with utter passivity. Paul threatened to set
fire to her father's closet of rifles, put a lit match to her hair and split
her lip with a punch. Mathilde gave a full account of these events and,
as her friend François Porché observed, she was 'totally lacking in
imagination, even of the most banal kind.' At the end of December it
was Arthur's turn to misbehave at a dinner of the Naughty Chaps.
Accounts differ, but during a reading of poems by a poetaster he
exclaimed 'Shit!' more and more loudly at the end of each line. When
Carjat remonstrated, Arthur lunged at him with Paul's sword-cane,
perhaps cutting his palm. He was calmed down by an athletic blond
painter, Michel de l'Hay, who took him to his studio to spend the
night. Paul called de l'Hay 'a very young man, among the most
remarkably handsome ever seen' and Lepelletier affirmed that de l'Hay
was a 'superb chappie;' since all it took was a blond hunk to calm
Arthur, his violence may again have been put on. His moody act as
frowner-with-a-knife did not please the Naughty Chaps, and he was
disinvited to future dinners. Paul was obliged to pay for more of his
meals, which may have caused a strain, as Arthur wrote to him soon
after, 'When you will see me positively eating shit, only then will you
no longer find that I cost too much to feed.'

On January 8, 1872 Paul rented a room for Arthur on the rue
Campagne-Première in Montparnasse. Five days later Paul attacked his

wife and hurled his infant son Georges against a wall which the baby hit with his feet, falling back safely into the crib. The Mauté family did not call in the police, probably from fear of public scandal. It is noteworthy how often Paul avoided police intervention after his violent episodes, no doubt due to his social status: when later he abandoned his bourgeois privileges, his relations with the police would change. Mathilde fled with the baby, saying she would return only after Arthur had left town. Characteristically, she complained not only about the new friend's violent influence, but also Paul's hygiene: he had taken to wearing old mufflers and, like Arthur, who considered body lice an amusing matter, rarely changed his shirt and underwear.

Paul convinced Arthur to return to Charleville at the end of February or the beginning of March as a sign of goodwill. By this time Paul was more concerned with remaining in contact with his son than in preserving his marriage. With Arthur away, Mathilde, from a mixture of naiveté and concern for public propriety, returned to her husband on March 15. At home Arthur expressed his anger by scrawling on park benches, 'Shit on God!' Delahaye wrote later that Arthur was worried about setting back his literary career by the untimely retreat, although he did write four poems under the title, 'Holidays of Patience'. In the first poem, 'May Banners', he asked the goddess Venus to pay less attention to shepherds 'who are more or less killed by the world'. The shepherds in question have been taken to mean V&R and their impeded love was one of the concealed subjects of the third poem, 'Eternity' in which Arthur tells himself, 'Here you leave off from human approbation and usual urges and you fly off accordingly.' In the last poem, 'Age of Gold', he braced himself for 'certain tortures' in his chosen destiny.

Before entering into the couple's further activities, it would be well to examine what evidence exists about their sex life. Wystan Auden wrote that 'all "abnormal" sex acts are rites of symbolic magic' and to understand personal relationships one must know 'the symbolic role each expects the other to play.' Most writers on V&R have implied that Arthur was the 'masculine' rough-trade top while Paul was the 'feminine' bottom. Jules Renard jokingly asked in his *Journal* if the 'Verlaine child resembles Rimbaud', suggesting that Arthur was the inseminator of the two. A letter from Paul dated May 18, 1873 confirmed this view, stating, 'I am your old cunt ever open or opened, I don't have my irregular verbs here;' the words 'old cunt', 'ever open' and 'opened', are in English in the original. Paul had written to Lepelletier from London in October 1872 that in pubs one could hear women address their men friends as 'old cunt'. Calling himself Arthur's 'old cunt' was an amusing catch-phrase but there was seduction too in reminding him of his penetrability. Paul's poem 'The Good Disciple' dated May 1872, ends with another invitation to penetration, 'Climb on my backside and throb'. Perhaps because of such availability, Nouveau called him in mock-Latin, 'Verulanus'.

But Arthur was not always eager to penetrate Paul, according to the Goncourt *Journal,* full of nasty but accurate gossip about writers' private lives. At a symbolist banquet, the novelist Alphonse Daudet recalled twenty years later 'the cynicism of Rimbaud's words shouted aloud in the middle of a café which said about Verlaine, "If he satisfies himself on top of me, fine! But doesn't he (also) want me to work out on top of him? No, no, he is really too dirty and his skin is too disgusting!"' Another Goncourt *Journal* story also described Arthur in the receptive role in anal sex: the gloomy, Poe-obsessed writer and musician Maurice Rollinat told Goncourt that 'Rimbaud, Verlaine's lover, that glorious one of abomination and disgust, who arrived at a café and laying his head on the marble of a table, shouted loudly, "I am killed, I am dead. Xxxx fucked my ass all night long ... I can't retain my fecal matter any more."' To the Goncourts writers often spoke in private about gay matters but shouting in public was definitely taboo. The physiological detail of anal sex followed by diarrhoea is also suggested in Arthur's poem 'Young Guzzler', in which Paul was penetrator: 'Cap/ of silk/ prick/ of ivory/ Garb/ very black/ Paul spies/ the armoire, / projects/ little tongue/ over a pear/ readies/ his *baguette* / and diarrhoea.'

More evidence of their sexual tastes may be found in Arthur's three poems grouped as *Les Stupra*, from the Latin word meaning defilement, although this title was given by its editors, not by the author. They were first published in 1923 when the Surrealists took an interest in his erotica. The poems are unabashed celebrations, not without humour, of a variety of gay sex acts, ranging from oral-anal contact to a suggestion of coprophagia. The first *Stupra* sonnet, 'Ancient animals bred even while running', was about phallic pride in ancestors who 'showed off their members proudly by the fold of the sheath and grain of the scrotum.' In the Middle Ages, a 'solidly hung fellow' was needed. He joked about a statue of the Napoleonic General, Kléber, that even though 'his pants seem to deceive a little, he probably wasn't lacking in resources'. Sizing up the basket of a dead general's statue was a camp joke but the final point was serious: 'no one dares erect his genital pride in the bushes any more where joking childhood is teeming.' Arthur was asserting his right to show off his erection: when he stayed in an attic room above Banville's apartment, chambermaids in rooms across the street complained about his antics by the window, and though he explained to his host that he merely took off lice-ridden clothes because he did not want to infest the room, this does not ring true from a youth so unconcerned with hygiene. To shock Parisian chambermaids he would have had to do something more than standing naked at a window.

The second *Stupra* sonnet, 'Our buttocks are not (like) theirs', described the difference between male and female arses, with the poet in the role of voyeur. A paradise of the flesh was evoked in the last lines: 'Oh to be just naked, seeking joy and rest/ Forehead turned to his glorious portion/ both free to murmur sobs?' The final question mark asked why this oral-anal stimulation should not be accomplished. One translator would exemplify the danger of inexactitude, especially with erotica, by rendering the line 'Our buttocks are not theirs' as 'Our arseholes are not like theirs'. Hearing about this innovative Englishing, the noted translator Richard Howard exclaimed, 'But that's the only thing that IS the same!' The poem was followed by the most famous *Stupra* poem, a collaboration between V&R, 'Sonnet to the Asshole'. It was written in response to a series of sonnets by Albert Mérat in homage to a lady's different body parts: her nose, lips, and cunt (politely spelled c— by Mérat), but omitting her asshole. Mérat had been admired by Arthur previously, but he failed to support the Commune, a fatal error. The 'Sonnet to the Asshole' is typically not included in editions of Paul's verse just as his pornographic 'Femmes/ Hombres' were omitted from the Gallimard Pléiade complete edition until the mid-1990s. Yet Paul wrote most of the 'Sonnet to the Asshole': his eight lines evoked a poignant tenderness with words like 'humbly', 'gentle' and 'tears'. The first line was 'Dark and wrinkled like a purple pink (*'oeillet violet'*) with *'oeillet'* meaning anus in the gay slang of the time, according to Alfred Delvaux's *Dictionnaire érotique moderne*. Arthur's final six lines were forthright and aggressive: there were sobs as in 'Our buttocks are not theirs' but of physical satisfaction. With his genius for ending poems memorably, he described the 'tube descended by the celestial burnt almond', suggesting a turd eaten by a lover. Even as readers of Sade, V&R's friends had never proposed coprophagia as a lovely thing for men to do. Because these poems were not published until decades later, they cannot easily fit into a history of the prosecution of other so-called 'immoral' works of literature, such as Flaubert's *Madame Bovary* and

Baudelaire's *Les Fleurs de mal*. The *Stupra* poems belong to quite another universe, a place where all can be said and experienced without boundaries. Flaubert would tell the Goncourt circle about wanting to describe a brothel of boy prostitutes in *Salammbô*, which in the end he did not do, and would read with great emotion the detailed confession of a gay murderer who strangled his lover out of jealousy and was guillotined at Rouen. However, speaking about gay subjects to a circle of friends, and immortalizing them in poems were different things.

Reactions were lively: In 1877 Rollinat wrote to a friend that the 'Sonnet to the Asshole' showed 'to what point the abuse of absinthe can go, the inspiration for this odiously pederastic sonnet.' When he wrote the letter, Rollinat was cleaning up his own act from Bohemian days to marry a respectable woman. By contrast Verlaine sent the sonnet to a friend on December 25, 1883 as a sort of Yuletide greeting. Steve Murphy has praised the sonnet as 'that exquisite *fleur de mal* born out of the love of two great poets, the only one they created together.' Part of the poem's beauty is in its abstraction of language; the asshole becomes a metaphor, an occasion for poetic inspiration: it is a tube, a 'feminine Canaan'. This has confused at least one critic, Enid Peschel, who stated that Paul's lines refer to a male asshole while Arthur's are in homage to a woman's asshole, although a preface to her book by Etiemble rejected this odd suggestion.

Generally, critical commentary on the *Stupra* poems has been obscured by most academics' discomfort with the subject. In her study *The Symbolist Movement*, Anna Balakian referred to V&R's 'abysmal homosexual adventure' adding that the poets' names were linked 'for reasons that are tragic'. Others have been similarly incapable of seeing any pleasure or fun in the relationship. Robert Greer Cohen wrote in *The Poetry of Rimbaud* of the two men: 'Their homosexual ménage was typically – as in Genet – unbearable at times, with sleepless Bohemian nights spent in mutual torment.' The generalization about Genet, a career criminal, and the idea of a 'typical' gay relationship remind us how rarely writers on V&R have dealt sensitively with these issues. Petitfils' biography stated that Paul had a homosexual 'tendency' but that Arthur 'had no taste in that direction, no leanings', and only agreed to gay sex as part of 'the rational disordering of all the senses'. Yet expressing his sexuality as a gay man, these sonnets are full of pride, joy, and poetic mystery. More evidence may be found in *Hombres,* Paul's collection of fifteen poems assembled while at the Broussais Hospital in 1891. Without it we would have lost vital clues about V&R's physical relationship. The Spanish word for 'men' was used jocularly for that language's sexy, macho qualities. His friend Cazals explained in *The Last Days of Paul Verlaine* that some of the *Hombres* poems date back to 'the terrible year' or 1873 1874 spent in jail, and were composed 'out of defiance or playfulness'. Speaking of *Hombres,* Paul claimed that 'erotic poems are written with a certain conviction and with more pleasure than the others'. He believed that 'lewdness' was an art form which one day would occupy 'an honourable rank between dance and music, beside poetry and painting.'

The first poem in *Hombres,* 'O do not blaspheme poet, and remember ...' compared men's and women's buttocks, as in Arthur's sonnet 'Our buttocks are not theirs'. The two poems seem part of a poetic challenge as in the collaborative 'Sonnet to the Asshole'. Paul didactically named a series of past lovers of the male arse, among them Shakespeare, the Valois kings, Louis II of Bavaria, and the city of Sodom, which 'died a martyr for its glory'. He stressed that he had sampled both men's and women's asses and the sister collection to *Hombres, Femmes,* included eighteen poems, which was slightly more than the gay-themed verses. Arthur, however, never achieved this virtuosity in bisexuality, nor was he as exuberant in heterosexuality as in homosexuality; he may well have had heterosexual experiences but they left hardly a trace on his life and art, apart from a possible infection with syphilis. A well-established convention of gay erotica is the praise of a partner's genital size: in *Hombres* Paul vaunted one lover who, although 'a boy, is hung like a man', just as in 'Ancient animals bred even while running' Arthur expressed similiar tastes. In their actual relationship, however, if Arthur did indeed prize a partner with large genitals, he might have been disappointed in this respect as far as Paul was concerned, as a medical report discussed in the next chapter makes explicit.

In the seventh poem of *Hombres* Paul described the joy of oral-anal contact as evoked in 'Our buttocks are not theirs'. Unlike the more fastidious Arthur in the Goncourt *Journal* quote, he was not at all offended by 'a little shit and cheese' in a male lover's unwashed bottom because he so loved 'to *gamahuche*', which is a rare verb he may have found in Victorian pornography. Paul's poems reflected a constantly shifting erotic focus as opposed to Arthur's steady fixation on the male body. The sixth poem of *Hombres* asked a male lover to 'climb on me here like a woman I fuck like a boy', creating a complex eros of ambiguity.

A Cavafy-like glow of past erotic satisfaction imbued the eleventh poem in 'Hombres': 'In that café jammed with imbeciles, we two ...' which is about masturbation while seated at a table. The two men are hidden 'by the clouds from our pipes', a hint that the masturbatory partner was Arthur, always depicted in caricatures surrounded by a cloud of pipe smoke. The exhibitionist theme from 'Ancient animals bred even while running' is recalled, since clouds of pipe smoke cannot really hide two men wanking in a café. The poem exulted in the public display and verbal invention V&R devoted to sex, using the unusual verb '*ingaguer*' or 'to defy', to describe how the lovers despise café patrons with 'their normal loves and fake morality'. Their penises were likened to 'the joyous nose of Karragheus', characters in the puppet theatres of Constantinople described in books by Nerval and Gautier. In 'A Heart Beneath a Cassock' Arthur used the Baudelarian word *'dictame'* or 'remedy' and Paul used the same word in the third poem in *Hombres* to describe the penis as 'nectar and "dictame" of my soul'. Sex was an excitation for the poetic process and occasion to coin new phrases, following Arthur's command that 'love is to be reinvented'. The critic Jean-Pierre Giusto wrote that 'homosexuality takes its place in Rimbaud's work as part of a demand for the total man, a new body finally capable of being a loving body, calling for a love that is celebrated in chorus, in freedom and unrestrained creativity.' Yet here, too, other scholars have disagreed, like Henri Peyre, who in *La Littérature symboliste* uncharitably declared, 'One would wish that (Verlaine) had died before the sordid decadence of his last years, and in fact we wouldn't have lost anything not to have *Hombres*.'

Their repertoire of sexual acts also included S-M knifeplay, with Arthur as aggressor and Paul as thrilled recipient. Antoine Cros, Charles' brother, told about the time in a café when Arthur said, ' "Put your hands on the table, I want to show you an experiment." They did, thinking it was a joke. Drawing a knife from his pocket, he cut the wrists of Verlaine deeply. I had the time to pull my hands away and wasn't hurt. Verlaine went out with his sinister companion and received two other knife wounds in the thigh.' Significantly, Arthur called this cutting an 'experiment' just as he had when he poured acid in Cros' beer in a café one day, mocking Cros' preoccupation with science. After the cutting Arthur and Paul went off together, which suggests that it was a collaborative venture, a deliberate show. Like other S-M enthusiasts, the two went shopping for equipment and prepared their play scenes. Delahaye reported that they 'bought sharp knives to fight duels in the style of German students'. They wrapped the cutting edges in cloth napkins so that only the points emerged and aimed for the face and throat, but 'their equal inability for cruelty prevented them from striking to kill ... If a little blood flowed, they soon ran to make it up over pints of bitter ale or brandy.' Unlike Delahaye, most friends were more offended by the knifeplay than by any other sexual aspect of their affair. It was a low-class activity, not for genteel people who preferred formal duels if violence was required. Knifeplay would cause them to be recalled in the Goncourt *Journal* as 'pederastic assassins', critizing Paul more for being cut up in public by a friend than for beating his wife and mother in private. As a didactic example of reinvented love, their sexual relationship had to be played out on the public stage with friends' noses rubbed into it.

Yet Paul cared very much about social acceptance and included Arthur when, soon after his arrival, the Naughty Chaps regrouped into a body known as the Zutiste circle. The name derived from the mild French expletive '*zut*', like 'Gosh-darn'. They wrote verses to amuse each other in a notebook, the *Zutiste Album*, like the one by the Naughty Chaps, later destroyed. The Zutistes, Jean-Louis Forain, Raoul Ponchon, Jean Richepin, and Maurice Bouchor, would be on good terms with Arthur for a time. Many writers are too hasty in depicting Arthur and Paul as total outcasts, and it is worth looking in some detail at their friendships. At least one of these friends may have been Arthur's lover.

In the Goncourt *Journal* story about Arthur's having sex with 'Xxxx', the four x's used to indicate the penetrating partner did not refer to 'Paul', since he was already identified as Arthur's lover and their liaison was so notorious that any attempt at anonymity would have been ludicrous. The all-night sexual partner whose name contained four letters must have needed a blind. One possible candidate is 'Jean' or

Jean-Louis Forain, only one year older than Arthur, who shared a room with him in the rue Campagne-Première. Forain needed anonymity later after he had married and enjoyed a bourgeois life. Goncourt would have protected him because they were friends as arch-conservatives: at the turn of the century Forain published many anti-Dreyfusard caricatures in right-wing journals.

A photo of the teenaged Forain shows him in picturesque artist's garb with a head of hair like a paint brush that justified his nickname, 'Gavroche' after the urchin in Hugo's *Les Misérables*. Years later at a lunch attended by François Mauriac, when asked what Arthur was like at this time, Forain replied, 'like a large dog'. Paul would call Forain 'my little brown girl cat' praising him for his obedience as opposed to the savage 'little blonde girl cat' Arthur, saying 'When I'm with the little brown girl cat, I'm good because the little brown girl cat is very sweet. When I'm with the little blonde girl cat, I'm bad because the little blonde girl cat is ferocious.' Forain drew a caricature of Arthur with the head of a cat and body of a jaguar standing on its dangerously muscled hind legs – a predatory feline. Because Forain would sometimes run after girls, Arthur called him 'young dog'.

In a number of memoirs and biographies he stated that in the room they shared there was only one bed, so Arthur slept on the bedsprings while he took a straw mattress on the floor. Forain repeated this detail until he seemed to protest too much. He may indeed have shared the mattress with Arthur, which would explain his later vehemence in declaring that Arthur was 'filthy' and claiming that he had told Paul, 'Your type of love disgusts me ... You talk about an ideal, a communion of minds ... (and here an unprintable word),' added one biographer.

In his haste to cover up the past Forain also possibly lost Arthur's

'Spiritual Hunt', reportedly one of his most accomplished poems. He recalled, 'Rimbaud stank of genius, he really did, he was wonderfully clever ... I had some manuscripts of his and some of Verlaine's and I'm sorry that I didn't keep them. When I went into the army, I entrusted Rimbaud's to a sort of actor-writer who didn't return them to me, and I found them again at Barthou's.' The 'sort of actor-writer' Bertrand Millanvoye sold the manuscripts as soon as they were worth something to Louis Barthou, a Paris manuscript dealer. Paul accused his wife's family of destroying it but his accusations against them are not always reliable. In her memoirs, Mathilde stated that none of Arthur's poems were ever stored in her father's home and it would be more reasonable to look for them in the apartment on the rue Campagne-Première, which does make sense.

Other clues about V&R's erotic relationship may be found in what remains of their letters: Mathilde was explicit about having burned a 'whole correspondence' from Arthur after Paul's death, forty letters at least, so that her son Georges would never read them. If she burned them around 1896 she must have quoted from memory in her book written in 1907–1908. Paul had asked Arthur to write 'martyrized' letters to him at home so that his wife and her family could see how he was suffering, while secretly writing to him in care of his mother about their future plans together; this would be a typical approach for Paul. In London he asked his mother to write letters which he could 'show to Arthur' and other secret ones with news of his wife. Missing letters have created textual problems: one which Arthur wrote in April 1872 was lost and remembered only because Mathilde stated that it included the phrase '*M— pour moi*', or 'shit on me', followed by the repetition eight times of the '*mot de Cambronne*', a euphemism for 'shit'. Editors have taken this to mean that the phrase '*merde pour moi*' was monotonously repeated eight times whereas the word '*merde*' only may have been repeated or scattered through the letter. Paul was usually playful in writing to friends and his letters to Arthur are especially encoded, using fake 'primitive' language of the 'Me Tarzan you Jane' variety. He gave male friends feminine nicknames, so that Delahaye became Delahupette, perhaps a play on the French term '*tapette*' or 'queer'. Other names have baffled scholars, such as in a letter of May 1872 telling Arthur: 'Me had 2 times last night dreamed: "You martyriser of children, you all *goldez*."' He added in a footnote that '*goldez*' could be written '*doré*' in English. Rather than the French word *doré* (gilt), he may have meant the artist Gustave Doré whose engravings Arthur loved and who in 1862 had made a lithograph, 'The Ogre', of a monster who looked eerily like Verlaine slitting the throats of sleeping children. This engraving or perhaps a Massacre of the Innocents in Doré's Bible Illustrations became part of their private erotic vocabulary: in the same letter Paul wrote, 'As soon as you return, take me in your fist right away.'

This erotic discourse was accepted by the couple's Zutiste friends, such as Ponchon and Richepin, whose tolerance was linked to their political radicalism, their resistance to the monarchy and conventional morality. A small but loyal circle of friends remained constant through all the public scandals. These friends were in turn rewarded by the rare privilege of being confided in by Arthur, who gave them copies of his work, and controlled his temper in their presence. What qualities did these faithful friends share? All were certainly tolerant about Arthur's sexuality, even if not themselves gay. Some published texts that subverted conventional views of sexual morality, either with humour or earnest argument: Ponchon, six years older than Arthur, was a lifelong bachelor who behaved like Auguste Bretagne, a typical gay café denizen of the time. Ponchon's *la Muse au Cabaret* contains a phallic poem in the *Zutiste Album* style that, like Arthur's *Stupra* poem, 'Ancient animals ...', was jokingly admirative of phallic size. 'The Sausage' was written to thank a 'certain Count' who sent Ponchon a ...

MAGNIFICENT ARLES SAUSAGE ... WHOSE PHALLIC FORM

WOULD MAKE MELANCHOLIC

AN ABELARD, MY DEAR

WHEN I COMPARE MYSELF

TO THIS UNUSUAL SAUSAGE

I FEEL A KIND OF SHIVER

AND DISAPPROVE OF MYSELF.

BESIDE IT I FIND MYSELF

QUITE A LITTLE BOY

WHAT AM I SAYING? GOD DAMN ME

IF A MULE'S THING

DOESN'T SEEM A TOY BY COMPARISON ...

WHAT FIG LEAF

HOWEVER FAT AND WORTHY

COULD EVER COVER IT?

An even closer friend was Jean Richepin, five years older than Arthur, who in the 1870s served a month in prison for publishing licentious verses. One British observer described Richepin's typical entrance into a Paris café: 'A magnificent specimen of manhood, facially and bodily like a warrior-figure for the antique Greek friezes ... His splendidly shaped lower limbs were cased in tight-fitting cashmere breeches ... the human athlete was accompanied by a canine one, as lithe and supple as his master ...' He even outdazzled pretty girls, the observer noted: 'a comely young woman, particularly neat and trim, passed unnoticed between the two of us.' Richepin was attracted to Arthur's 'angelic eyes, unforgettable eyes', and called him a 'good poet, better than good, but what an awkward customer *(mauvais coucheur).*' Richepin was open-minded about gay friends and a story, 'Good Prostitutes' from his *Truandailles* describes a gay street-singer seducing prostitutes by his appearance, yet showing 'a despising turn of the lip that said very clearly, "It isn't for you that the oven heats up, my little

kitties."' They invite him upstairs for free sex but he refuses, finally
admitting, 'I don't like that. I'm like you, I only love my little man.'
The story concludes with a kind of respect for the gay singer: 'It was
said in such a convinced tone and one felt so surely that he loved in
his own way, passionately and madly, that some whores murmured,
sobbing, "Poor love, go along with you."'

Richepin offered more explicit arguments for tolerance to gays in an
essay on Sappho in his *Grandes amoureuses*, pointing out that instead of
accusing Sappho of 'criminal' acts as a lesbian, one must recall that she
lived ...

> ... *among the Greeks ... Touched by beauty, a Greek didn't even seek to know if it
> was of one sex or the other: he simply loved. We know Plato's theories on this
> subject and the example of Socrates himself proves that the Greeks had no scruple
> in practicing what the Symposium defined. So why be offended or surprised by
> Sappho's loves which are simply the complement of Plato's loves. No, there is no
> crime. There is only a difference in morality. Therefore, it is not a question of blaming
> or defending Sappho. We only try to understand ...*

He may have had in mind Paul's poem, 'Ballade Sappho' defending
homosexuality in which he stated repeatedly, 'I am comparable to the
great Sappho.' Richepin's understanding must have gratified Arthur
who gave his friend one of the first printed copies of *A Season in Hell* –
Ponchon got one too – as well as manuscripts from *Illuminations*.
Richepin later recalled that he had owned letters from Arthur, some
illustrated with caricatures, a notebook with sketches for poems, and
one filled with 'rare words, flashes of rhyme'. Richepin explained that
the 'very curious' letters 'disappeared from my papers' as had those
from Paul and Nouveau. As a member of the French Academy in later
years he may have destroyed the letters as too compromising.
However, five pages of aphorisms survived, written in 1875 by

DETAIL OF RIMBAUD, FROM FANTIN-LATOUR'S 'COIN DE TABLE'

Richepin, Nouveau, Ponchon, and other friends and this *Richepin Album* included an identification of poets as sexually ambiguous: 'During my voyage to the planet Saturn I saw some men dressed as women. As I looked somewhat surprised, I was told, "These are poets."' The author of 'Saturnian Poems', Paul, was referred to here along with other colleagues.

Another friend tolerant of V&R's behaviour was Maurice Bouchor, a poetic prodigy born in 1856 whose first book, *Joyous Songs*, appeared in 1874. Remembered today for the earnest verses that inspired

Chausson's 'Poème de l'Amour et de la mer', Bouchor also wrote jolly odes to drunken revelry with pals like Ponchon whom he praised as 'a pagan whose goddess is Joy', declaring, 'I love you as much as pale ale.' He wrote lyrics about the joys of the open road, such as 'Wandering Players': 'To the road, all poets/ to live in eternal holidays./ Through stupefied cities/ Let's pass like a flight of larks,' and the love for footloose camaraderie kept him friendly with V&R after they ran away to Brussels, while his writing career thrived as Arthur's shriveled and died.

These friends' sexually free jokings have been preserved in the *Zutique Album*, a book in the tradition of priapaea. Parody verses, many of them obscene, were crammed onto pages decorated with drawings of penises of various shapes and sizes. Paul drew caricatures of little men with swollen, dripping penises. Another technique was to trace one's finger on the page and sketch in detail making it look like a monumental penis. In one aphorism Paul altered a statement from one of Molière's plays, 'Polygamy is a case, a case that can be punished by hanging (*un cas pendable*)' to 'Pederasty is a case, a case that can get a hard-on (*un cas bandable*).' Léon Valade wrote a verse satire on a gay priest: 'If the flesh feels troubled/ to see two lovers chatting, forgetting the time/ we have as comfort the interior joy/ of being able sometimes in remote corners/ to spank little boys with their pants down.' As illustration Paul drew a priest with a hard, dripping penis, its tip darkened in.

Arthur was one of the most prolific contributors to the *Zutiste Album*. In two poems, 'Paris' and 'Lines for Places' he mentioned the French mass-murderer J-B. Troppmann who was guillotined in January 1870 for killing a family named Kinck and whose crimes triggered the establishment of a popular press in France because so many people were so eager for news about him. Henry James's *A Little Tour in France* describes how in that year *Le Figaro* was filled with 'descriptions of the horrible Troppmann, the murder of the *famille* Kink (sic). Troppmann, Kink, *le crime de Pantin* – ... Had I abandoned the sonorous south to associate with vocables so base?' Arthur, however, was thrilled by such vocables and several others also associated him with the famed killer. The essayist Léon Bloy wrote in *le Chat Noir* in 1884 that Rimbaud 'resembled a murderous young velocipedist, something like Troppmann in the flower of his adolescence.' Lepelletier in *l'Echo de Paris* in November 1891 also stated that Rimbaud reminded him of Troppmann and, like him, was expected at some time to be guillotined: 'his head would fall aureoled in glory into the infamous basket.'

The Zutistes were therefore chosen friends with specific views in common, unlike the men V&R were grouped with in Fantin-Latour's famous painting, *Table Corner*, an idealized image of the couple that became the one most often reproduced for posterity. This uniting of V&R was probably Paul's idea, just as he had asked Carjat to preserve Arthur's beauty in photos, although Mathilde later claimed that he merely used the posing sessions as an excuse to be absent from home. Fantin was a painter of unexciting still lifes and group portraits, and his Arthur does not resemble the photos which have survived; instead the inspiration seems to have been Caravaggio's boy prostitutes with their symmetrically round faces crowned by bouffant hair and their favours symbolized by still lifes of fruits, flowers, and wine. Fantin's Arthur has a still life of flowers over his head and wine nearby. Forain sketched him as a Coreggio-style cupid, with the inscription 'Who rubs against him gets stung'. More than portraits, these were cultural commentaries on the eroticized adolescent in the Italian Renaissance tradition of ambiguous sexuality. Both Fantin and Forain ironically expressed the difference between the sweet exterior and ferocious inner person, and Fantin complained that the angelic-looking sitter's filthy hands had to be washed before each posing session.

The grouping of writers in the Fantin portrait was originally intended to include Mérat but he refused, apparently not because of the 'Sonnet to the Asshole' but rather Arthur's sword-cane incident. His place was taken in the composition by a large bouquet of flowers. According to the Goncourt *Journal* of March 18, 1872, other writers also declined to pose for Fantin because they didn't want to be painted in the company of 'pimps and thieves'. The painting was exhibited in the 1872 Salon where it was reviewed in *Le National* by Théodore de Banville, who noted that Fantin 'bestowed in advance the laurels of history painting on some very young poets of indisputable talent' like 'Arthur Rimbaut (sic) a very young man, a child the age of Chérubin, whose comely face wears an expression of astonishment under a wild, tangled mop of hair, and who one day asked me if it would not soon be time to abolish the alexandrine!' Few thought at the time that the Fantin portrait would become an icon of the gay couple, representing an idyllic moment of their relationship – a couple soon to encounter fatal problems because of the differences in their personalities, as well as the disapproval of the outside world.

By May Arthur had returned to Paris and Paul was attacking his wife again. Arthur constantly changed lodgings until June 15 when yet another violent scene occurred between Paul and his wife. On July 7 the two men left Paris together. At the train station in Arras the police were called when they were overheard joking in loud voices about imaginary crimes they had committed, Arthur going on with relish about 'strangling an old woman'. This provocation was probably in response to local people staring at their shabby appearances, but the joke would have been funnier had not Paul in fact been recently strangling Mathilde. They were sent back to Paris but made good their escape via Charleville on their way to Brussels where they arrived on

July 9, 1872. A week after leaving and wanting to keep lines of contact open with his son, Paul wrote to Mathilde that his sudden disappearance was only 'a bad dream' and one day he would return. Thinking of her 'duty' rather than pleasure, Mathilde decided that she had to try to reclaim her husband and travelled to Brussels with his mother to persuade him to leave with her for New Caledonia, where many Communard exiles lived. These 'very interesting personalities' such as the socialist Louise Michel could be interviewed for a project Paul often spoke of but never wrote, a history of the Commune. Mathilde convinced him to board a train to Paris but he stepped off at a station en route and returned to Arthur, sending her a note decrying her as a 'miserable carrot fairy'. Subsequently, Paul wrote her an even more bizarre letter, inviting her to live with them, and mentioning 'Rimbaud who is dressed in velvet like a simple Sivry, has lots of success in Brussels and would be very happy to have you with us.' She did not take the bait. On September 7 V&R left Belgium for England, arriving at Dover. It is unclear why they left the congenial atmosphere of Brussels, although some Communard exiles there were unenthused about the lovers' S-M routines. They had not managed to earn a living in Belgium and the possibility of perfecting their English in the land of Shakespeare must have been attractive.

Arthur wrote a poem, 'Holidays of Hunger', in which he addressed his poverty in London, 'My hunger, Anne, Anne, flee on your donkey ...' He focused on the near-homonym in French of woman and hunger (femme and faim) as more than coincidental. His poems from this time spoke of an inevitable study through which he hoped to be a master of happiness by using magic charms: 'O seasons o castles! What spirit is flawless? ... Long live happiness each day when in the morning the Gallic cock sings.' The bird exuded national pride, but also sexual potency. 'Comedy of Thirst' expressed the desire for alcohol, but also for water, knowledge, and freedom in a questing mode. Alcohol also played its role in 'Good Morning Thoughts', an invocation to Venus, asking the goddess to bring alcohol to 'charming workers'. There was as ever the mystery of the literal meaning of his lines: 'Wandering Jews of Norway/ Tell me the snow/ Dear ancient exiles/ Tell me the sea.' The fact that *Norvège* (Norway) and *neige* (snow) rhyme is significant, but not decisive: the rhyme was anything but gratuitious, instead seeming part of a bardic incantation, a poetic charm with the power of prayer to match his aspirations. And as so often, there was an echo in Paul's poetry when he later referred to the couple as 'Good wandering Jews' ('*bons juifs errants*'), also a reference to a popular serial novel by Eugène Sue. Their hurtlings around were still providing poetic inspiration but in London the two would find that their love affair was at the beginning of its end.

PAINTING BY JEF ROSMAN. THE TEXT IN THE PAINTING READS 'FRENCH-STYLE
EPILOGUE /PORTRAIT OF THE FRENCHMAN ARTHUR RIMBAUD, WOUNDED AFTER-
DRINK BY HIS INTIMATE THE FRENCH POET PAUL VERLAINE/ FROM LIFE BY JEF
ROSMAN/AT MRS PINCEMAILLE'S HOUSE, TOBACCO VENDOR RUE DES BOUCHERS
IN BRUSSELS'.

Getting rid of Verlaine: 1873

Alternately manic and depressed in London, Paul revelled in Arthur's company, but also wanted to hang on to his family connections as husband and father, which was clearly impossible. The conflicts caused by his actions made for wide mood swings, accentuated by substance abuse. Both men kept up a heavy consumption of drinks and drugs in the place Paul called 'incredible city, black as ravens and noisy as ducks'. Paul later commented on how many scenes of vomiting he'd witnessed. When Delahaye came to visit he found Arthur in a hashish stupor, complaining that he had seen no visions apart from moons pursuing one another. Yet throughout their London adventures Paul wrote letters to his friend Lepelletier which show an exuberance in contrast to Arthur's sullen moods. Paul wrote in November 1872: 'I take the opportunity of this letter to curse as one must the abominable oxtail soup. Fie on such a horror! A man's sock with a rotten clitoris floating in it. There is also the coffee, PLAIN per cup, a horrific mix of torrified chicory and milk which evidently comes from Father Mauté's teat. Fie on such a horror! And then Gin! It's anisette drawn from a vulture's single bollock.' The same letter revealed a roving eye:

> Bathrooms in cafés are called lavatories because there are faucets, sinks, and soap in the place itself. When you go out, you fall right into the hands of young boys who for two sous, brush you from head to foot: For a little more, I don't know what they must do for those in the know, but they have a mightily suspicious appearance with their clinging little suits and their generally charming faces.

He wrote to Lepelletier in December about a new male friend he had met: 'I believe I've found something very sweet, almost childish, very young, very candid, with amusing and charming brutalities and gaities. To find that, you must dig arterial wells.' By then the V&R relationship was apparently not exclusive, if it had ever been so.

Paul knew that Mathilde's family was organizing a legal separation and was moved to propose to Lepelletier with bravado in a November 14 letter that V&R undergo anal examinations to 'prove' that their relationship was non-sexual: 'If necessary we are ready, Rimbaud and me, to show our cunts (virgin) to the whole group.' Lepelletier advised him not to volunteer for physical examinations, no doubt aware that such an exam would produce incriminating results, as indeed a mandatory one did soon afterward. But for the moment they were on an emotional high, which included viewing Fantin's *Table Corner* on display in London: 'We just came from seeing ourselves. It was bought for 400 pounds (10,000 francs) by a man rolling in money from Manchester. "Fantin for ever!," ' Paul exclaimed, with the last phrase written in English. Soon after Arthur left for France, perhaps another case of putting on a good image for Paul's upcoming legal battle. He admitted to Lepelletier that he was feeling 'very sad: all alone. Rimbaud, whom you don't know, whom I am the only one to know, is no longer here. Terrible emptiness! The rest doesn't matter to me. It's smut.' Paul's mother visited him, her presence being 'very useful to me from the point of view of "respectability" ' using the English word in the original.

Although in search of respectability, Paul explained in an October letter that 'as for love here, it seems that ladies' ten fingers play a greater role around insular penises than the *barbatum antrum*.' He reported on British slang on November 14: 'Did you know, I've just learned from a "canny French fellow" that our *membrum sacro sanctum*, apart from names like prick, cock, wang, creator, sub-prefect, dick, weewee – the later two used by children – bone, member, thing, tail, etc. is also called turtle – the head of the cock. Hence these drawings.' He added three obscene sketches labelled 'Triple Demonstration By Way of the Fine Arts'. In December he offered details about the prostitution of her Majesty's Horse Guards: 'The grenadiers, splendid men in red, curled and pomaded, "give their arms" Sundays to ladies for an average of sixpence. But the Horseguards, breast-plated, booted, and in helmets with white tassels – a shilling! Boy!' Paul described areas like Haymarket which were interesting 'turally', meaning for finding '*cul*' or 'ass'. 'The Widow Fist reigns on these orgiiies! (melody by Gounod),' he wrote, again implying that prostitutes preferred to masturbate their clients.

From such manic jokes he soon fell into depression: in January he suffered a sort of seizure and wrote to his mother and his wife that he was dying. Mathilde didn't open the letter but Madame Verlaine arrived and paid for Arthur's ticket as well. Paul recovered rapidly and from January through March, V&R lived together again in London. Their British friends included the poet W.E. Henley, who later 'recounted enormities' about the two lovers to Paul Valéry 'in slang of a surprising crudity and authenticity'. On April 3 they left for Belgium again. Paul later wrote to his friend Emile Blémont that 'in London I owed my health only to the caring of my mother, combined with the admirable devotion of Rimbaud, who came back especially from Charleville.' Paul was unnerved by his wife's legal action and planned to return to France to fight. A week later Arthur was at Roche but by May they were together in Belgium. The back-and-forth nature of the relationship was growing tiresome.

V&R were both very difficult, if not impossible, people to live with, each with his private obsessions and aims. Both abused drink and drugs, and their lives were often made physically uncomfortable by sheer poverty. Paul's emotional inability to let go of his wife and child added further pressure to an already shaky friendship. Mutual contempt flourished under these conditions, and we find scattered references in the couple's letters to things that irked them: Paul's habit of drinking in the mornings offended Arthur, who preferred to stay sober until after a day spent studying at the library. Arthur's constant anger at everything and everybody was tiresome to Paul's softer, more yielding temperament.

Many writers have tried to find more concrete causes for the breakup. Cocteau later wrote that in London Arthur was disappointed to find that he was living with 'a man who drank and who was very, very weak in a certain way, and not after all the male he'd thought, the god Pan he'd thought – it was the man of the hidden poems, of Hombres.' Blame for Paul's drinking and pornography was curious coming from Cocteau, a former opium addict who wrote the erotic *Livre Blanc*. The problems were more fundamental: different priorities, different ways of working or not working; their love had developed into incompatibility.

Isolated in the countryside, Arthur planned a 'Pagan Book or Nigger Book' as he wrote to Delahaye in May 1873, which would develop into one of his most remarkable works, *A Season in Hell*. In the same letter he punningly expressed his boredom, the 'contem-prostate of nature absor-buttfucking me completely.' ('*la contemplostate de la Nature mabsorculant tout entier.*') Yet at the same time that *A Season in Hell*, a nine-part poem mostly in prose, was taking shape, he was also slowly compiling the forty-two sections of prose poetry that would result in his final masterwork, *Illuminations*. Much ink has been spilled over which work he wrote first, where, and when. It seems likely that in 1873, both works were on his mind, whereas *A Season in Hell* was dated by Arthur as written from March–May 1873. Work continued

GETTING RID OF VERLAINE: 1873   65

on *Illuminations* until 1874 or 1875. Critics have tried with varying success to link certain parts of the poems to periods in London or Brussels, but their hypotheses, however well-argued, remain just that.

A Season in Hell was a kind of rap in today's sense of the term with overtones of the rhetorical tradition of sermons by Bossuet and Lammenais. A highly theatrical monologue, it benefits from being read aloud. Flashes of wit and irony highlighted the monologuist's command of his rant. The poem's intellectual ambition embraced history, science, sociology, myth, race, the conflict between East and West, work, politics, economics, all in concise form. With daunting mental command, the poet played with key words and catch-phrases from his life with Paul. Putting words in the mouth of one's beloved is a common literary habit as in Stein's *Autobiography of Alice B. Toklas*. *A Season in Hell* proved how closely Arthur had listened to Paul's way of speaking, his ideas and reactions. The measure of Arthur's disappointment was in relation to the hopes he had pinned on his lover. Without Paul's presentation to literary Paris, he might not have tried as long as he did to prepare books for publication and even fewer works would have survived. As it was, their love inspired not just *A Season in Hell* and *Illuminations* but also Verlaine's finest collection, *Songs Without Words*, apart from numerous individual poems.

The nine sections of the poems comprise a Preface, followed by sections entitles 'Bad Blood', 'Night in Hell', 'Ravings I: Foolish Virgin, Infernal Bridegroom', 'Ravings II: Alchemy of the Word', 'The Impossible', 'Flash of Lightning', 'Morning' and 'Farewell'. In grim, sardonic prose poems, interrupted only rarely by metric verse, Arthur recounts a solitary trip to hell, during which he tried to reinvent everything anew. Despite the first person singular, the poem's narrator is not meant to be taken as a literal portrait of Arthur, yet there are many correspondences. At times his choice of words reflects his reading, ranging from the Bible to Edgar Allan Poe, as the mighty problems of sin, God, and how to live are weighed one after another.

His tough, somber text is challenging and polemic, with a valedictory tone, a *nunc dimitiis* that had been heard in 'The Drunken Boat' and would reappear later in *Illuminations*. The poem included a monologue by a 'Foolish Virgin', a character named from the medieval French parable of the Foolish and Wise Virgins. She describes her 'hellish bridegroom' who states, 'I don't like women. Love must be invented afresh, that's for sure.' He announces, 'I am going to make gashes all over my body, and tattoo myself, I want to become as hideous as a Mongol. You'll see, I will shout in the streets.' They are a *'drôle de menage'*, an odd pair, who exchange 'piercing caresses'. The love in the Foolish Virgin's monologue is part of a series of quests for knowledge and experience and the tragic tone implies that they have failed. The rhythm is inexorable and the word choice inevitable, the real challenge of a prose-poem since strict metrical rules do not apply. The prose passages are broken by metered verse that are mystical chants, spells with incantatory power.

The power and range of the writing is astonishing, yet the message is one of a man certain that he has failed in everything he has tried, especially in the creation of a new poetic language. To Arthur, his 'disordering of the senses' was a fiasco, but posterity has judged his efforts in a dramatically different way. The very accent on solitude suggests that by the time he began writing *A Season in Hell*, Arthur realized that Paul's company alone would not solve the major problems of his life. The difficult, angry teenager saw himself as doomed to go it alone.

By contrast, Paul was as jokey as ever in letters to friends, and as devoted to Arthur. On May 16 Paul wrote to Lepelletier from

London, claiming, 'Alas, I'm chaste ... since leaving Paris,' and the editor of his correspondence, Van Bever, admitted having cut 'eight words in which the author testifies in very lively terms to his virility.' He added on May 19 that he was 'very much attached' to dedicating his book, *Songs Without Words*, to Arthur: 'First as a protest and because when these verses were being made he was there and pushed me a lot to make them and above all, as testimony of gratitude for the devotion and affection which he always showed and particularly when I almost died. This trial must not make me into an ingrate, do you understand?' Lepelletier thought such a dedication would be prejudicial, but Paul replied in a May 23 letter that the 'crafty tittle-tattle' would continue anyway and claimed the poems signified nothing 'inphamous' or '*infemme*' (not about women). He cited a few poems which could stand as 'testimony, if need be, rather in favour of my perfect love' for women. He asked, 'How is it audacious to dedicate a book which is in part travel impressions to someone who accompanied you during the impressions received? But I repeat, if you prefer, cut it, censor friend.' The dedication was finally omitted.

On 27 May V&R were in London trying to find work as French teachers, but on July 3 they quarrelled when Paul returned home with a herring for their dinner: Arthur said, 'If you knew what a cunt you look holding that fish.' Paul threw the fish at him and walked out, arriving in Brussels on July 4. Perhaps he believed he could influence Mathilde by again separating from Arthur, who wrote a pleading letter: 'Come back, come back, dear friend, my only friend, come back.' The end of the letter is arranged like a free-verse poem:

YES IT IS I WHO WAS WRONG

OH YOU WON'T FORGET ME, SAY IT?

NO YOU CAN'T FORGET ME

MYSELF, I ALWAYS HAVE YOU HERE

SAY IT, ANSWER YOUR FRIEND, ARE WE NEVER TO LIVE TOGETHER AGAIN?

BE BRAVE. ANSWER ME QUICKLY.

I CAN'T STAY HERE ANY MORE.

JUST LISTEN TO YOUR GOOD HEART

QUICKLY, TELL ME IF I SHOULD REJOIN YOU.

YOURS FOR ALL MY LIFE, RIMBAUD.

The critic Henri Guillemin wrote harshly that the letter showed the 'manners of a slut left by her protector because she went too far in insolence and who promises to be gentle and nice if the gentleman will take her back.' But clearly sincere, Arthur wrote the poem 'Shame' which reproduced the emotional mood of the quarrels, calling himself the 'troublesome child' who disturbed the marriage. He explained that a foolish animal must always deceive and betray 'like a Rocky Mountain cat, stinking up all the spheres!' Identifying with this cat, Arthur invented his own term for the Rocky Mountains, '*les Monts-Rocheux*' instead of the standard '*les Montagnes rocheuses*'. He ended the poem with a brief prayer recalling his childhood plea for mercy for François Villon. Arthur now fully realized the emotional toll of a poet's life, and Paul, who had always been difficult, became impossible with his indecisiveness and sloth, getting drunk mornings 'when left to his own devices'. At first Arthur had accepted to share Paul's indecisions about his wife and child but in the long run he became tired of the situation.

On July 4 Paul wrote to his mother, to Madame Rimbaud and to Mathilde, asking them to join him in Brussels in three days or he would commit suicide. Mathilde no longer read his letters, but Madame Verlaine arrived by the July 5. The next day Paul wrote to Lepelletier stating again that he planned to kill himself and asked him to supervise the publication of *Romances sans paroles*, poems partly inspired by Arthur. On July 7 he sent a telegram announcing his decision to enlist in the Spanish militia to Arthur, who arrived that evening, and the next days were spent in quarrels and discussions. Arthur explained to Paul that he intended to leave for Charleville or Paris, as both men now realized that they could no longer live together. The violence that would soon break out was thus not rationally linked to their continuing as a couple, since that was over, by mutual consent. The events do seem dream-like, as recounted in various depositions with varying degrees of candour. Paul had threatened suicide so often that Arthur may not have realized the full depths of his despair this time. It may also be that through their frequent separations, Arthur had acquired a certain distance or remove from which he could pitilessly judge Paul's emotional states. This distance might have made it difficult to predict just if and when Paul would finally turn his threats into action.

The shooting incident which followed has attracted a great deal of attention over the years, although so many details are debatable that a full investigation would require a book of its own. It was one of a series of s-m incidents with the usual tormentor and victim's roles reversed. On July 10 Paul bought a 7mm pistol with a six-bullet capacity and fifty bullets, and explained when asked by Arthur what it was for, 'It's for me, for you, for everybody.' The irrational response of a drunken man who was depressed about the permanent alienation of his wife and child. Indeed, the final realization that he had lost wife and child may have weighed on him more than any estrangement with Arthur, as the latter had gone off and returned so many times before. No doubt in response to Paul's hysteria, Arthur was even more pitilessly bullheaded than usual, offering arguments to Paul's maunderings. When Arthur insisted on leaving him to his own thoughts in the hotel room, Paul fired two shots at very close range, wounding Arthur once in the left wrist. He felt immediate remorse and asked Arthur to shoot him, which he declined to do, instead going to the hospital to have the wound bandaged, telling doctors that the shooting was an accident.

Once again, Paul almost escaped serious punishment for an act of violence. He was apparently allowed to keep his gun, and Arthur simply insisted on leaving as a way to close the incident. Around 7pm, Arthur headed for the Gare du Midi accompanied by Paul and his mother. En route Paul put his hand in his pocket and showed signs of impending violence, or so his estranged friend feared. The actual danger of more shooting at that point is impossible to discern, but perhaps, had Arthur been emotionally closer to Paul at this point, he might have read his mood more accurately, and the police would never have been the wiser. As it was, Arthur ran to a policeman in the street for protection. Paul was arrested and sent to the Brussels' Amigo Detention Center, an ironic name for its friendly connotation and his belief that Spanish was a sexy language.

On July 11 Arthur entered the hospital again to have the bullet extracted and the next day testified in favour of Paul, asking that charges be dropped. Two days later a surgeon reported on the wound at the Saint-Jean Hospital: 'Its form is round, edges bruised and torn, diameter about 5mm.' He left the hospital on July 20 and while recuperating in a Brussels boarding house was painted by a young artist, Jef Rosman. Signed and dated, the oil on a panel of acajou is inscribed on the white screens around the poet's bed, 'French-style epilogue / Portrait of the Frenchman Arthur Rimbaud, wounded after-drink by his intimate the French poet Paul Verlaine/ from life by Jef Rosman/ at Mrs. Pincemaille's house, tobacco vendor rue des Bouchers in Brussels.' The waggish inscription informed Belgians what French friends did to each other and insisted grandly that the scene was painted 'from life', unaware that posterity would treasure this record of a moment in literary history. When the previously unknown painting turned up in a Paris antique shop in 1947 some experts could not believe it was authentic but today it is universally accepted. Arthur was shown in Paul's usual role of feminized 'victim', Like the story of the infant Paul's blood staining a bedsheet, the red quilt that covers Arthur's lower body has a menstrual connotation. His head leans on his right hand in the pose of Saturn whom Paul had identified with in 'Saturnian Poems', The irony of presentation notwithstanding, it is a desolate scene: Arthur's mouth is an unhappy crease and Rosman positioned himself beneath the level of the bed to see into his subject's slit-like eyes. Unlike photographs in which his eyes reveal nothing, here they are forced open by reality, like a dog photographed using a flash, astonished at the intrusion into his privacy, a further violation after the shooting itself. Paul may have requested this portrait of Arthur, since he was at the origin of most of the others.

The Judge ordered the court physicians to examine the prisoner 'Paul Verlaines' for 'any traces of pederastic habits'. Doctors Vleminckx and Semal reported, in a file that remained unpublished until 1985:

> 1. *The penis is short and not voluminous, the glans is especially little and it narrows, tapering off toward the end, starting with the crown. The latter protrudes little and does not have a marked relief.*
>
> 2. *The anus can be dilated rather significantly by a moderate separation of the buttocks, to the depth of about one thumb. This movement displays a tunnel-shaped flaring, a sort of shortened cone, with its top portion below. The folds of the sphincter have no lesions and bear no marks ... The contractibility remains more or less normal.*
>
> *C(onclusion): This examination shows that P. Verlaine bears on his person the signs of active and passive pederastic habits. One and another of these two signs are not strong enough to create the suspicion of inveterate, old habits but more or less recent habits.*
>
> *Brussels July 16, 1873.*

In 1985 the Belgian Ministry of Justice refused to allow the scholar Françoise Lalande to reproduce the document in facsimile, which she suggested showed a 'bad conscience. The Brussels file is damaging, certainly, but to whom?' Paul was likely shaken by this exam but he wrote at least nineteen poems during his first three months in jail and after he was allowed books, studied Shakespeare and Don Quixote in the originals. He planned a poetry collection, 'Cellulairement' and continued to admire, love, and respect Arthur, if not in exactly the same way as before. Among the poems he wrote in prison was 'Crimen Amoris', a highly coloured scene set in Ectabana, where an Evil Angel, a beautiful sixteen-year-old boy, burns a palace of orgies during a Festival of Seven Sins – a mythologization of Arthur who, Paul implied, was guilty along with himself merely of 'crimes of love'.

Mathilde later wrote that Paul did his best work while in prison or hospital and some academics have oddly agreed: In 1950 the critic Martin Wolf wrote, 'Probably the greatest misfortune ever to befall Paul Verlaine in his tragedy-riddled career was the fact that he was sentenced to only two years in jail – instead of life imprisonment – for the attempted murder of Arthur Rimbaud.' Practically speaking, prison meant that for years he was not welcome to publish poems in major Parisian literary reviews. While he remained in custody, the Paris police were asked by the Belgians for further information and in response, a report dated August 1 described 'the Parnassian poet Robert Verlaine', and said that the shooting followed a fight 'about money' between Verlaine and 'his girlfriend Raimbaud'. The poet's marriage ...

> ... went rather well despite the mad crazes of Verlaine whose head had long been unhinged until Misfortune brought to Paris a kid Raimbaud (sic) born in Charleville ... In terms of morals and talent this Raimbaud, aged 15 or 16, was and is a monstrosity. He possesses the mechanics of verse like no one else, only his

works are absolutely unintelligible and repugnant. Verlaine fell in love with
Raimbaud who shared his passion and they went to Brussels to taste heart's peace
and what ensued ... The lovers were seen in Brussels practicing their loves openly.
Verlaine told his wife, 'We, we have the loves of tigers.' And saying this he showed
his wife his chest tattooed and wounded with knife cuts which his friend Raimbaud
applied. These two beings fought and tore each other apart like ferocious animals in
order to have the pleasure of making up again.
    Police Report. Officer Lombard.

In her memoirs Mathilde stated adamantly that her immediate family
gave no information against Verlaine to the police, but other witnesses
were plentiful. Auguste Mourot, a relative of Madame Verlaine and an
art student in Brussels, blamed Paul's imprisonment on Arthur's
influence and told the police they were lovers. Paul asked to confess to
a Catholic priest and when a Father Descamps arrived he began to list
his sins until the Belgian finally interrupted, asking, 'You've never
been with animals?' On August 8 he was sentenced to two years in
prison and a fine of two hundred francs. The maximum sentence
should have been eighteen months but the judge tacked on another six
months because he had supposedly 'deprived a worker of his ability to
work'. The sentence was confirmed on August 27 and the poet was
transferred to Brussels' Petits Carmes prison.

Back at the family farm in Roche, Arthur shut himself in the attic and
finished *A Season in Hell*. In prison Paul continued a warmly nostalgic
view of their love but Arthur was ever-critical, trying to learn
definitively from their relationship as a thing of the past. In another
poem probably written after the shooting, 'Brussels', Arthur referred
to 'the little widow's cage', just as Paul described himself as a widow
in *A Season in Hell*. The atmosphere of 'Brussels' was uncanny calm
after a tragedy as life goes on: 'calm house, ancient passions'. He
described himself wandering about unbelievingly, which is how he

arrived at Roche from Brussels, where all he said about the shooting was to moan, 'Oh, Verlaine, Verlaine!' Arthur gave *A Season in Hell* to a printer in Brussels; his mother covered the down payment after he showed her the work. Whatever Madame Rimbaud thought of it, an emergency measure like paying for publication was needed to advance her son's literary career, mired in scandal after Paul's imprisonment. She had been receiving anonymous letters revealing the true nature of Arthur's relationship with Paul, although she publically pretended to be unaware. She did, however, pay a visit to Mathilde, asking her not to continue her lawsuit against her husband, as the results might reflect badly on Arthur. Mathilde incredulously recalled, 'I received her politely, but ...'. On October 22, Arthur returned to Brussels to pick up a few advance author's copies but the rest of the edition remained at the printer's until it was rediscovered in its original packing in 1901. He deposited one copy inscribed 'To P. Verlaine', at the Petits Carmes Prison and in Paris on November 1, gave copies to such friends as Ponchon and Richepin. The book did not attract a single review and he quickly returned to Charleville where he spent the winter. Still, his literary career was not quite over and his most majestically confounding work, *Illuminations*, was yet to be completed.

Travels of 'Thing': 1874–1875

With Paul in jail and *A Season in Hell* published, Arthur worked on his series of prose poems *Illuminations*. Divided into forty-two sections, this great work is an eternal puzzle in that, as Enid Starkie put it, 'the words mean little in themselves, and their real value lies in their spontaneous power of suggestion.' Under such headings as 'After the Deluge', 'Childhood', 'A Tale', 'Parade', and 'Antique', the sections represent a further step towards personal isolation: instead of the heated autobiographical tone of *A Season in Hell*, here we have a series of withdrawn portraits, as formally daunting as Bach's *Art of Fugue*. Like a portrait painter who decides to devote himself to landscapes, Arthur in *Illuminations* took a step away from human likeness.

Illuminations remains as disconcerting to read today as it must have been to see the first abstract paintings for those who expected subject matter in art. The forty-two prose poems on the themes of the city, travel, theatre, war, a new form of love, nature, water, and boats are still dazzling, but also baffling: the critic Jean Starobinski confessed that he never wrote about Rimbaud because he didn't understand *Illuminations*, and the mighty poet and translator Marie Ponsot refused a publisher's commission to produce a literal translation of the poem because 'there is often no single English word that can say what each French word means.' In the prose poem 'Vagabonds' there is a 'pitiful brother' and a 'satanic doctor', the latter dreaming to restore his friend to 'his primitive state as Son of the Sun'. He told of 'vaguely hygenic distractions' after which the 'poor brother' would get up 'screaming his idiotic dream of chagrin'. Paul took this to be a reference to himself but like the Foolish Virgin in *A Season in Hell* this was not meant literally. Murphy wrote that the *Illuminations* are 'deliberately caricatural and marked by polemical fervour: Rimbaud addresses an argument to his friend full of hyperbole and allegory.' A riddle poem entitled 'H' has been interpreted as about masturbation, called 'Hortense' like Paul's camp joke of giving names to inanimate objects – he called the manuscript of *Songs Without Words* 'Gustave', referring to it as 'this frail boy'. In 'Tale' Arthur spoke of himself as a prince or genius who had reinvented love, presumably with Paul. In 'Lives' he spoke again of the 'key to love' and in 'Royalty' V&R were implied in the phrase 'sons of the sun'. 'Sentences' offered parodies of the way Paul spoke while in 'Workers' he was renamed Henrika in camp fashion. Although the relationship with Paul was over, Arthur was still using terms that reflected gay concerns. In the prose poem 'Parade' he referred to young men with 'frightful voices' sent into a city 'to take it from behind, got up with disgusting luxury.' The prose poem 'Devotion' referred to a heart made of 'amber and spunk', spunk being a slang term for sperm even in the nineteenth century.

Critics have suggested that at least seventeen of the forty-two prose poems contain references to Paul and their love affair. Despite attempts at relationships with Forain and Nouveau, no one else could touch his heart and this may have sealed his poetic fate. In the prose poem 'Lives' in *Illuminations* Arthur referred to 'five or six widowhoods', implying that he had that many failed relationships, all with men: Paul, Forain, Nouveau, Cabaner, perhaps Delahaye, and even Bretagne. These elements argue that homosexuality was not a passing experiment for Arthur, but something ingrained in his mind and heart.

Paul's collection, *Songs Without Words*, also referred to their relationship, although in a typically more upbeat way: the poem, 'It's the langourous ecstasy', could be read as a nineteenth-century version of Auden's 'Lay your sleeping head, my love ...'. Another of his 'forgotten ariettas' inspired by a favourite author of Arthur's, the eighteenth-century librettist Favart, began with a plea for indulgence for the two travellers. 'You see, we must be pardoned things ...' Paul believed that the poet was a privileged being who should be allowed more license than ordinary mortals, while Arthur darkly saw the poet's suffering as immense and inevitable. Another epigraph, 'The King's conquests', evoked the conquering spirit the lovers felt as they travelled in freedom, exulting in their love. A poem dated August 1872, set in a bar asked, 'Hasn't our love/ found its niche there?' The poem 'Spleen' apparently described one of Arthur's gloomier moods. Through mighty efforts, Arthur would manage to get rid of Paul, but the reverse was not possible. While languishing in prison, Paul was told that Mathilde had been granted a legal separation, whereupon he turned to Catholicism, perhaps to avoid sharing Arthur's pessimism.

In late March 1874 Arthur ran off to London with Germain Nouveau, a gifted young poet and member of the Zutistes circle. When Arthur proposed to Nouveau that they go to London, he agreed so quickly that by mistake he took along the key to his Paris hotel room and left important papers behind. Friends were convinced that this was a new 'drôle de ménage'. Richepin later recalled that Arthur, 'still far more famous for his adventure with Verlaine than for his works, had begun to visibly dominate Nouveau, who had a weak nature and exalted character, and the nervousness of a sensual woman abandoning herself to someone strong ... It looked very much like a rape-kidnapping (enlèvement).'

The new companion was three years older than Arthur, small, infantile and often hysterical. He was born with the medical condition monorchidism, meaning he had only one testicle or as he wrote in a poem, 'I have only one dubloon in my purse but it is a very good one.' 'The Refusal' declared Nouveau's bisexuality: 'I am a pederast in my soul/ I say it aloud and standing erect/ But lying in your bed, Madame/ I wouldn't say it any more.' He spoke of a 'pretty school' of pederasts and added, 'My word, / I don't yell at my friends' with the verb *engeuler* playfully changed in the sentence from *enculer* or 'I don't fuck my friends in the ass.' He protested against critics of pederasty who had a bad effect on male friendships: 'Passing for only half a man/ wouldn't I have the right, in sum/ to seek to complete myself?' The poem had conviction despite its irony, like his parody in the *Zutiste Album* of Paul's lyric, 'Your soul is a chosen landscape': 'Your soul is a Colbert that costs two *louis*', the Colbert being a whorehouse next to the Bibliothèque nationale. Nouveau described the 'unbelievable angels' there who, 'while keeping a Hindu calm ... suck you off with a gentle gesture/ and their odour mixes with the blasts of pricks/ the abrupt blasts of pricks, so clever/ that they make souls fall down in ecstasy.' Gay jokes were part of his sensibility: in a letter written from London to Richepin, he exclaimed about a red-coated soldier on parade, 'Oh, the pretty red *queue* he has in the back, the gentleman!' which can translate as 'tail in the back' or 'prick in the backside'.

Nouveau brought something of Paul's humour and animation to the new couple, but if anything he was even more infantile and unstable than Arthur's previous companion. Work on *Illuminations* continued and the two friends gave lessons in French and drawing. On April 4 they received reading cards for the British Museum Library, Arthur again lying on his application that he was over twenty-one. He stayed in London until the year's end. Nouveau returned to Paris in June, perhaps not because of their poverty, as has been suggested. He was so extreme that mere starvation would not have put him off, but Arthur's single-mindedness while writing *Illuminations* must have been difficult to live with. Nouveau never forgot their adventure and later wrote

'Song of My Adonis' in which Echo spoke of a lost adolescent love:

AT 15, A YOUNG MAN MY AGE
CAME ONE DAY TO TELL ME, 'LOVE ME!'
THAT WAS THE ONLY MARRIAGE WE HAD
JUST LIKE WHAT GOES ON IN THE FOREST.
… ADONIS WAS MY MAN'S NAME
AS FOR ME, THEY CALL ME ECHO
THE FUNNIEST THING WAS, AT BARS
HE NEVER PAID HIS SHARE.
AFTER FOUR MONTHS OF LIVING TOGETHER
ONE FINE DAY, NEAR THE OPÉRA
HE TOLD ME, 'I'M LEAVING ON A TRIP.'
PROMISE ME YOU'LL WRITE
HIS ADDRESS DID NOT ARRIVE QUICKLY
IT GOT LOST, I SEE
THE HARDEST THING IS THAT BY FLEEING
HE LEFT ME ONLY MY VOICE.
ALL MY JEWELS TOOK OFF
I'VE MOURNED MY WATCH
NOT EVEN A POCKET HANDKERCHIEF IS LEFT
TO WIPE MY LITTLE EYE!

Arthur was not fifteen but nineteen when he ran off with Nouveau, but looked younger and had the habit of being treated at bars. Taking all their possessions was characteristic, although to leave a poet with his 'voice' is not negligible and the 'little eye' wiped in the final line may refer to *oeillet,* the gay slang term for anus, affirming what friends suspected about their sexual relationship.

Nouveau later wrote other poems about the breakup, including 'Lost Poison': 'From the nights of the blond man and brown beer/ nothing

« L'HOMME AUX SEMELLES DE VENT »

'LAY-TUST' NEWS: RIMBAUD CARICATURED AND MOCKED BY VERLAINE, 1875

remained in the room/ Not a piece of summer lace/ not one shared necktie.' After their tryst Nouveau may have also had a sexual relationship with Paul. He competed with Paul and Delahaye over who could make the best drawings inspired by Arthur's travel experiences. The three-way exchange of caricatures expressed a shared physical and emotional experience, betraying an attachment to the subject and emotion that underlies the humour. Caricaturing Rimbaud was a way to grasp the absent body, preserving its image. Although comic in intent, it was akin to the Roman Emperor Hadrian's commissioning memorial portraits of his lover Antinous. The sketches of Arthur emphasized his long legs and childish face and he was frequently shown nude – undressed after being robbed in Vienna, with the naked chest and small nipples of a boy, or draped in a filmy diaper as an angel outside a bar crowning a friend with laurel. People who knew the group had little doubt of their shared sexual experience; as one friend, Eugène Guerrin, implied, writing that Nouveau 'wouldn't have been the friend of Verlaine and Rimbaud without moral flaws, sometimes prolonged ones. Like the dog in Scripture, he returned to his vomit.'

Alone in London in mid-June, Arthur advertised in the British press for work and for three days *The Echo* announced: 'A Young Parisian – speaks *passablement* – requires conversations with English gentlemen; his own lodgings, p.m. preferred – Rimbaud, 40 London-St. Fitzroy-Sq. W. 18.' The French word for 'passably well', was used probably not because he forgot the English (as critics have claimed) but to please the British taste for reading a few catch-phrases in French. At the British Library he asked for Sade's work but the staff, willing to bend the rules to admit a reader under twenty-one, would not give him banned books. Inside the BL he possibly sat near Karl Marx, another habitual reader at that time.

Ever the student of languages, he made a list of English phrases that caught his attention which if read selectively tell an emotional tale:

HEARSE – HEARSE CLOTH – THE THROBBING OF THE HEART

HE WOULD NOT HAVE THE HEART TO DO IT ...

IT LIES ON MY HEART – I HAVE NO HEART FOR IT.

HEART BREAK HE WEPT HEARTILY ...

HEDGEHOG – TAKE HEED – SHOW US YOUR HEELS ...

HE HELPED HIMSELF TO THE BEST BIT

WHAT A HELPLESS BEING ...

TO FLY OFF THE HINGES – SPEAK OUT, I DO NOT TAKE HINTS

I HAVE HIM ON THE HIP — HIPSHOT — ...

THESE MANNERS OF HIS WILL — THERE IS A HITCH ...

THE THING WAS BLAZED ABROAD AND FAILED

YOU MUST LEARN TO ABSTAIN FROM THESE INDULGENCES ...

NO MAN'S FACE IS ACTIONABLE ...

THIS MAGGOT HAS NO SOONER SET HIM AGOG, THAN

THE NEGOCIATIONS WERE AGROUND ...

ALRIGHT — ALLURING — ALM — ALMOND

TO WALK ALONE — IT IS BETTER TO LET IT ALONE

HAVE YOU ALTERED YOUR EXERCISES?

NOTHING COMES AMISS TO ME ...

DO YOU NOT ANTICIPATE MUCH PLEASURE

I NEED NOT APOLOGIZE — APPENDAGE ...

AS YOU LOVE ME, DO NOT ATTEMPT IT ...

I ASK NOTHING BETTER THAN TO GO — TO LOOK ASQUINT ...

THEY BAFFLED ALL OUR DESIGNS

THE SKIN BAGGED — WHAT DO YOU BAIT WITH

WE ALWAYS BAIT AT THAT INN.

It may be read as a source list for his emotional state after the ruined affair: feelings include grief and despising ('what a helpless being'). A 'maggot' or strange obsession was used as a euphemism for homosexuality in Sylvia Townsend Warner's later novel, *Mister Fortune's Maggot*. A shooting, 'manners' being 'blazed abroad' like their affair, 'indulgences' which must be abstained from. Phrases sound like possible translations of their conversations: 'As you love me, do not attempt it ... I ask nothing better than to go.' The appendage discussed; the erring part which must be curbed; the baiting at an inn which may have been a favourite pub of Paul's — A friend, the sexologist Havelock Ellis, noted that Paul, too, attached ritual significance to certain English words in a way that puzzled native speakers of the language because he ...

... had a curious love for the plastic moulding of speech. Sometimes one would hear him mouthing some strange new word over and over on his tongue, shouting it in different tones, emitting it with sudden explosive energy as though to catch unaware its spirit, not resting until he had gained a mastery of its vocal value. So a dog will sometimes lick round and round a morsel of dubious value, until at last it gains a sweetness not its own which he has imparted to it, and he swallows it with gusto.

Despite his improving English, Arthur remained jobless and so he sent an appeal to his mother, who arrived in July with Vitalie in tow. Playing the tour guide calmed him until the end of July when he left to work at the port of Scarborough. By early November he was out of work and so advertised in *The Times* again. He finally completed *Illuminations* which was his farewell to literature. With *Illuminations* waiting to be recopied, Arthur returned to Charleville in 1874. He took piano lessons from a neighbour and left for Stuttgart the following year in order to learn German, soon travelling to Italy and hoping to go to Spain, also for language study. His travels were made difficult by a constant lack of money and the need to find employment, punctuated by illness. He never wrote any more poetry. The death of his sister Vitalie in 1875 gave him migraines and thinking to cure them he shaved his head, producing another opportunity for caricature.

On March 2 Paul, freed early after eighteen months of prison, found work as a teacher of French and drawing in England and later of English in France, although his pedagogic talents were weak. Mallarmé, a more serious English teacher, when asked later to offer a professional evaluation of Paul, wrote that he believed the way to teach French students English was to have them pronounce French with a caricatural British accent and so when he entered the classroom they greeted him, 'Baonn-jaur, Maossiun Voeu-laine!' Among the poems composed in prison was 'Poet and Muse' about 'a room on the rue Campagne Première in Paris in January 1872.' He revisited in memory the scene of their ecstasy and asked, 'Room, have you kept their ridiculous ghosts,/ oh full of filthy daylight and spider's noises? ... You do not understand anything about the things, good people/ I tell you that it is not what one thinks.' He had made a similar comment in a letter to Lepelletier: only he really knew Arthur, only he had really understood their love. He would see Arthur one last time in Stuttgart and obtains from him the manuscript of *Illuminations*.

In a letter of March 1875 Arthur told Delahaye that Paul, now derisively called Loyola because of his religious beliefs, had arrived in Stuttgart, 'a rosary in his paw' but that 'three hours later we had denied his god and made the 98 wounds of Our Saviour bleed.' There is a strong sexual connotation here, given their previous s-m habits. The use of the nickname Loyola is intriguing, since that saint converted while recuperating from battle wounds, whereas Paul became pious after inflicting mayhem on someone else. This, their last meeting, has usually been interpreted as a brawl with biographers using the '98 wounds' reference as proof. Some even went so far as to suggest that Arthur left him bleeding in a ditch. The novelist Stefan Zweig would later depict with gusto the Stuttgart reunion in a short book on Verlaine: 'In the flooding moonlight by the banks of the Neckar the two greatest living poets in France fell upon each other in wild rage with sticks and fists. The struggle did not last long. Rimbaud, athletic, like a wild animal, a man of passion, easily subdued the nervous, weakly Verlaine. Stumbling in drunkenness, a blow over the head knocked him down.'

However amusingly this reads, in fact anything but consensual rough-housing seems unlikely, as after they met Paul showed his continued goodwill by trying to arrange for the publication of *Illuminations*. He also wrote a tender poem about 'the sadness, the languor of the human body ...' a description of Arthur sleeping during the Stuttgart visit with his 'feet still painful from the road/ the breast, marked by a double punch/ and the mouth, still a red wound/ and the quivering flesh, frail décor/ and the eyes, the poor eyes so beautiful from which shine/ the pain of seeing again something that is over. Sad body! How weak and how punished!'

In September or October 1875 Paul addressed another caring, if chiding, poem to Arthur, whom he called 'unfortunate one!' because although he had 'all the gifts, the glory of baptism/ your Christian childhood, a mother who loves you ...' he had become a 'prodigal son with the gestures of a satyr'; he called upon the 'god of the humble, save this child of anger!' Outside of the poems, Paul kept his sense of humour about Arthur, asking friends for news about 'Thing' ('Chose') or 'How is Stuttgarce?', a pun on the city's name that means 'Stutt-bitch'. Letters and drawings by Delahaye kept him apprised of Arthur's movements: a caricature from October 1875 showed him tapping Delahaye's shoulder outside a grocery shop whose window displayed two huge ithyphallic artichokes. Paul received letters from Arthur requesting money with a hint of blackmail and replied assuring his friend of 'the same affection (modified) for you ...' but with exasperation at his 'perpetual anger against everything'. He refused the request for money for piano lessons, suggesting that Arthur ask his mother – which he surely knew would infuriate him – and concealed his address to prevent further blackmailing missives.

From this time, Arthur would be off on farther and farther travels. Some readers are curious about the writer's life after he stopped writing. But to study Arthur's activity in Africa in detail is like taking a writer who was crippled by a stroke and spent the rest of his life in front of a TV set and analysing the programmes he watched. In his book on the poet, Yves Bonnefoy refused to speak about the last years as of no public interest. We lack the documentary detail to understand what all scholars interpret as a loving relationship with his Abyssinian servant Djami Wadaï, which brought some light to an otherwise unrelieved picture. Therefore, the focus here is on his last years as they appeared to friends he left behind in Paris.

Arthur's abandonment of literature at age twenty or so has not surprised every writer: the French aphorist E. M. Cioran would write in his *Cahiers*:

> *In Rimbaud everything is unimaginable and abnormal, except for his 'silence' …*
> *Had he lived to be eighty, he would have finally commented on his explosions,*
> *explaining them and himself … Rimbaud's effervescent period should be imagined*
> *as an unusually long ecstasy but which once exhausted could by no means begin*
> *again. His 'silence' is only an entry into a different order of existence, in a state that*
> *one grasps better using categories of asceticism than those of literature.*

Georges Bataille's *Interior Experiment* also justified his silence: 'The refusal to communicate is a means of communication more hostile, yet more powerful, than any other.'

Travels beyond: 1876–1891 and after ...

In May 1875 Arthur was on his way to Siena when he suffered a serious case of sunstroke and was brought back to hospital at Marseilles. His next plan was to enlist in the Spanish royalist troops, but he did not succeed in doing so. Having recovered by July, he got a temporary job as tutor at a vacation class at Maisons-Alfort, a southern suburb of Paris. He even considered becoming a missionary in the Far East, another project that fizzled out. Instead he practiced foreign languages and the piano. Paul drew a caricature of him banging away on the keyboard to neighbours' distress under the slogan: 'music sweetens the morals'.

In 1876 he reached Vienna but was robbed by a coachman; without money, he was sent back to France. Delahaye sent Paul a letter heavy with sexual innuendo, first mentioning Nouveau, 'Squeeze at least his hand for me', and stating that Léon Valade, jokingly called 'VALARD' 'has a good time now and then with' Arthur, called 'Thing' in their private slang. This was done 'all the more easily as [Valade] married a nymphomaniac old tart of seventy – horrible scandal for his compatriots.' Whatever the relationship with Valade, Arthur was soon off to Brussels and in 1876 worked on a Dutch ship bound for Java via Southampton, Gibaltrar, Naples, Suez, and Aden in Abyssinia. In May 1877 he wrote in German-flavoured English to the American consul at Bremen, asking to join the American Navy. After more voyages through dozens of faraway cities and a brief return to Roche in 1878, where he helped his family with the harvest, he was off again to Italy, the Middle East, and Cyprus where he worked as an overseer in a quarry. By 1879, sick with typhoid fever, he returned to France, but was soon ready to leave again. However, he only got as far as Marseilles when typhoid obliged him to return home once more to recuperate. In March, 1880 he revisited Alexandria, Cyprus and finally Africa. All these travels were followed with amused fascination by friends in Paris who rarely went beyond their local cafés or the countryside for a holiday. Delahaye saw him in Roche in 1879 and noted that his previously fair complexion had changed to the 'dark skin colour of a Kabyle – and on this brown skin was a blond beard.' His voice too had changed: 'Instead of a nervous timbre that I'd known before, it had become serious, deep, impregnated with calm energy.' Two years later Delahaye would write to him in Aden and he responded with a long list of books he needed, addressing the letter by mistake to 'Alfred' instead of Ernest Delahaye. The latter was as obsessed as ever with Arthur and drew caricatures of him tattooed with images of pipes, absinthe glasses, and bottles. Arthur might perhaps have acquired some tattoos during his adventures as a sailor. But unlike Paul and Delahaye, today's readers do not have the option of amusement at these frantic voyages, knowing their tragic finale.

In the last dozen years of his life, Arthur worked in the import-export field for a series of French employers dealing in everything from porcelain to weaponry, running guns to fuel local wars. He did not trade slaves although at one point he sought to buy two for his private use, which is not much better, despite defences by writers who have disputed the myth of Rimbaud the slave-trader. His letters from Africa express almost unrelieved misery, boredom, depression, and no redeeming interest in the arts. In 1880, his first year in Africa, he was hired by a French import-export firm in Aden and on November 10 was transferred to Harar in central Abyssinia, a city with a population of around forty thousand. From then on his life was mostly a boring and infuriating mix of illnesses and frustrations. Although he wrote a report on one exploratory voyage to Ogadine, between Harar and the Somali Desert, published in 1884 in the minutes of a French geographical society, it would not be read today were he not its author.

Along with his literary silence, Arthur's formerly exhibitionistic sexuality became discreet. His 'five or six' relationships with men had failed and for a time he shared his home with a native woman before suddenly dismissing her when a business opportunity obliged him to travel. In September 1885 he wrote to a colleague that he had 'fired that woman in an unremitting way ... I've had that masquerade in front of me long enough.' She appears to have been more of an employee than a real companion. Henry Miller, who could be relied upon to recognize a heterosexual when he saw one, wrote that Rimbaud never loved women and the only person he may have loved was his African servant boy, Djami Wadaï. Djami's last name is rarely cited by writers, as if they had adopted colonialist ways in denying a native his full name. The good and faithful servant and possibly lover would be his major heir apart from his family.

Accounts of these years often imply that by going to Africa, Arthur became a macho man, abandoning effeminate ways such as homo-sexuality and poetry. Such authors ignore the tradition of gay explorers, naturalists, and military adventurers to which Rimbaud corresponded: Alexander von Humboldt, the Russian Nicolas Przhevalsky, Maréchal Lyautey, and General Gordon of Khartoum, to name just a few, brought their homosexuality to distant climes, driven by their countries' lack of acceptance. Claudel remarked to Gide that in Abyssinia when Arthur was there 'every officer without exception ... lived openly with his boy.' There are even signs of a certain feminization in Arthur's wearing native gowns and suggesting to a colleague, Ugo Ferrandi, that it was best 'to squat to urinate.'

Although Arthur had turned the page from his previous existence, in Paris his legend was not forgotten. Félicien Champsaur's 1882 novel *Dinah Samuel* included a character, Arthur Cimber, an unpleasant 'little thug' even if he was 'the greatest poet on earth'. But Arthur would soon be widely admired as a great modern poet due to the persistent efforts of Paul, and in a later edition of his novel Champsaur deleted the character, perhaps for fear of offending his admirers. In 1884 Paul published *Les Poètes Maudits*, including studies of Arthur and Mallarmé. Some critics have suggested that he used Arthur's work to reinvigorate his own career which had not recovered from the imprisonment scandal. It is more likely, however, from the run-on descriptions of his beauty, that Paul was instead trying to repossess Arthur in a lover's way. He described the Carjat photo of 1871 thirteen years later: 'A sublime child ... lips which have long been sensual and a pair of eyes lost in very ancient memory, rather than a dream, even a precious one. A kid Casanova but much more experienced in adventures ... this totally virile disdain for grooming, which is meaningless for what is literally devilish beauty!' Nearly a decade after he had last seen Arthur, Paul was still in his sexual thrall, seeing in the Fantin portrait 'a sort of glowing and smiling sweetness in these cruel blue eyes and this strong red mouth with a bitter crease: mysticism and sensuality, and how!'

At the same time, in his book *Parallèlement* Paul offered his frankest and most extended evaluation of his own gayness, comparing Arthur and Mathilde as lovers, with the former winning. In the poem 'Explanation' he recalled 'the joy of bleeding on the heart of a male friend/ the need to weep for quite a long time on his breast' and in 'Another Explanation' he praised their 'love that trickled with flames and milk'. His poetic activity was renewed, but Paul had not learned to control his domestic violence and a year after *Les Poètes Maudits* appeared he was sentenced to a month in jail for beating his mother.

He was freed in May, just as the final divorce from Mathilde came through. A compensation came in an unexpected good review for *Les Poètes Maudits* by the Catholic writer Léon Bloy in *le Chat Noir*: 'I like this mad enthusiasm ... It's a sort of testimony of the human soul, after all, and in this dog of a world there is nothing else worth walking three steps to look at.' Paul's 1886 preface to *Illuminations* presented Arthur as the son of good bourgeois parents instead of a satanic ephebe. Félix Fénéon reviewed the book in *Le Symboliste*, making fun of the idea of a bourgeois Rimbaud, but adding that he 'floats in a mythical shadow over the Symbolists' and praising *Illuminations* as 'finally, a work outside of all literature and probably superior to it all.' Téodor de Wyzewa, a musicologist, agreed, writing in *La Révue indépendante* in December 1886 that *Illuminations* was 'a perfect musical suite' and its author was 'such a prodigious soul ... a master who has no imitators.'

In September 1888, Paul heard the false rumor that Arthur had died. In response to this news Paul published in *la Cravache* a long poem 'Laeti et errabundi', about their 'joyous wanderings' when 'passions satisfied/ Insolently, beyond measure/ put holidays in our heads/ and in our sense, given assurance by everything .../ disconnected from pitied women/ and the latest prejudices.' He revelled in the memory of their bold trips, 'the novel of two men living together' even though they were 'not ideal spouses'. Paul addressed his lover: 'They say you're dead .../ I don't want to believe it,/ You, god among the demi-gods!' Arthur was his 'miraculous poem/ the complete philosophy/ my fatherland my bohemia/ Dead? Go on with you! You are living my life.' In February 1889 Paul published in *la Cravache Parisienne* an outspoken defence of homosexuality: 'These passions which they alone still call loves/ are loves as well, tender and furious/ with curious particularities/ which everyday loves certainly lack.'
In the wake of this publicity and the discovery of previously unknown

poems by Arthur, *Le Décadent* published a series of poems presented as his which were really written by the journalists Ernest Raynaud and Laurent Tailhade. In March 1889 the magazine printed a spoof that since Rimbaud had such a 'colossal' reputation abroad, many journalists in Paris were angry that there was as yet no statue of him in the city, so the editors proposed to erect one for the Universal Exposition. A week later, Paul published an open letter in *la Cravache Parisienne* to protest at the joke about 'a person who is absent, and what a person!' Tailhade confessed that he had written poetic fakes and the statue joke, but would now stop. But the April *Le Décadent* published a supposed list of donors to the monument including General Boulanger (500 francs) and the French President Sadi-Carnot (10 francs), and claimed that the poet, presumed dead, would be buried in the Panthéon. The forgeries had some impact: in September 1891 the *Revue de l'Evolution sociale, scientifique, et littéraire* published an article by Dr. Emile Laurent, arguing that Rimbaud was a madman, based on an analysis of two poems which had recently appeared in the press, both in fact forgeries by Tailhade.

Chuffed by the publicity, Laurent de Gavoty, the editor of a Marseilles-based review, *La France moderne*, got Arthur's address and wrote in July 1890, calling him 'the head of the decadent and symbolist school' and asking for a contribution to the journal. Surprisingly Arthur saved the letter. Gavoty bragged, only a week after he wrote it, that soon he'd publish unknown works and in February, 1891 he told readers that the magazine really knew where Arthur was: 'It isn't a Decadent's prank ...Who wants to bet?' The word prankster (*fumiste*) pursued Arthur to the end, describing his life and art. In 1890 Guy de Maupassant stated in *la Vie errante* that many people felt Rimbaud was only a 'prankster'. In the Goncourt *Journal* of February 1891, Rodolphe Darzens stated, 'Rimbaud is now a merchant in Aden and in the letters he writes, speaks of his past as an enormous prank.' (*fumisterie*). In fact his correspondence from these years is mostly humourless apart from an occasional nasty irony. Two of his colleagues, Armand Savouré and Alfred Ilg, corresponded in February 1888 about newspaper coverage of Africa and joked, 'It's Rimbaud from Aden who's amusing himself by writing pranks to the press.' Even Izambard wrote in *l'Echo de Paris* in December 1891, 'I'd swear that it was with an amused eye, with a good humoured Olympian laugh that he saw from the other side of the world all his admirers and devotees establishing rites in his honour.' But Izambard had not seen him for years, and the less people knew Rimbaud, the more they were likely to see him only as a practical joker. In 1893 the poet François Coppée published in *Les annales politiques et littéraires* a mocking poem: 'Rimbaud, successful prankster/ In a sonnet I deplore/ wants the letters O E I/ to form the tricolour flag./ In vain does this Decadent perorate/ We need without any ifs, ands, or buts/ a style clear as the dawn/ That's the way old Parnassians are ...'

Since no one except perhaps Djami Wadaï was close to Arthur, no one could see the full misery of his existence, which soon worsened. In February 1891 he felt agonizing pain in his left knee to add to his rheumatism, fevers, and other ills and wrote to his family, 'I figure that my life is in danger.' Years before, at age twenty-two, he had told Delahaye that he didn't expect to live beyond twenty-seven. Now he saw death approaching again and this time he was right. Rather than seek treatment for his painful leg, he decided to exercise it to the point of exhaustion. By the time he went to a doctor it was too late and bone cancer had spread. In agony he landed at Marseilles for treatment, but the only option was amputation. He sent a telegram to his mother, who came for a short time before returning to nurse Isabelle who was also ill. As soon as she was able, Isabelle came to Marseilles and accompanied him back to Roche, before he left once again for Marseilles. A doctor who saw him several times in Roche,

VERLAINE, WRAPPED IN A TYPICAL RATTY MUFFLER (ABOVE) PINES
FOR A SPLENDIDLY GARBED AND PIPE-SMOKING RIMBAUD (BELOW)

Henri Beaudier, recalled that the patient had a 'cold face, glacial', and
when asked about his poems replied, 'Shit'. When Beaudier asked
Madame Rimbaud why Arthur had left for Marseilles, she replied
violently that she had no idea...he had left English coins with his
mother to pay me.

In his final delirium Arthur thought of returning to Africa, but he could no longer escape himself by imagination or on foot. The obligatory military service was a torment to him until he was definitively excused. Isabelle was engaged to a rich local landowner, 'without distinction or intelligence' in a marriage arranged by her mother. She confided her uncertainties to Arthur and he 'violently made her reject such a marriage. No, she, so "interesting", so noble, so refined, could not marry such a gross man. He gave her the courage to refuse', a friend wrote later. Among other distractions one hopes, but somehow doubts, that he got a smile out of a letter in approximative French from a Greek business colleague at Harar, Dmitri Righas: 'Yu tell me that they did anoporation on yu, numbly that they cut orff yur leg and that stroke me very mutch, aswellas all yur freends in Harar. I wudda prefer that they cut orrf mein stedda yurs. I wush yu a girdle recovery ...'

His final days were described in many accounts by Isabelle, mostly unreliably, as she was driven to prove that Arthur was a holy Christian martyr. Biographers have lingered over his agony in a way that combines voyeurism with morbidity: when Arthur was in a relationship with Paul, he wanted to cry out his sexuality from the rooftops, but as a miserable dying man he only wanted, and deserved, peace and anonymity. He died on November 10, 1891 and was buried in Charleville in strict family intimacy. Two days later a collection of his poems, *Le Reliquaire*, edited by Rodolphe Darzens, was reviewed in *L'Echo de Paris* by a journalist unaware the poet had died. He told a false anecdote about Victor Hugo meeting Arthur, feeling his skull and declaring him a 'boy Shakespeare', to which he murmured, 'He bores the shit out of me, this old dotard!' Readers were also informed that he was 'today a slave-trader in Uganda'. The next day the newspaper announced that Rimbaud had taken a fall and by coincidence at the same time, 'his master Verlaine' was entering Broussais Hospital 'to have his ailing leg treated' – these poets 'are therefore truly *maudit*'. Rémy de Gourmont reviewed *Le Reliquaire* in *Mercure de France* in December, saying that the poet was as handsome 'as an appropriately pustulent toad or a lovely case of syphilis'. Yet the first review of *Season in Hell* appeared, in *L'Univers Illustré* of November 28, in which Anatole France praised the prose poems which had the 'balance, rhythm, and mysterious charm of the finest verses'.

Only in December was his death announced in a few newspapers and by then the myths had already begun. In an 1891 book, *Impressions and Opinions*, the Irish novelist George Moore wrote that he had been 'stabbed ... in a house of ill-repute' by Paul and had 'left Europe to immure himself forever in a Christian convent on the shores of the Red Sea; and where it stands on a rocky promontory, he has been seen digging the soil for the grace of God.' A French biographer of Moore suggested that he may have confused Rimbaud with Charles de Foucauld, a famous French missionary and martyr. In a later book, *Memoirs of My Dead Life*, Moore admitted he had been wrong but didn't bother to correct them for reprints of *Impressions and Opinions*.

While Arthur's life was ending, Paul was in Broussais Hospital in suburban Montrouge, which, according to his friend Adolphe Retté, was 'a heap of little buildings that evokes something like a Boer village'. There his poorest friends would visit at dinnertime to share the food. Two other visitors in January, 1890, André Gide and Pierre Louÿs, paid homage, finding him with an unbuttoned shirt revealing a fat white hairy chest. He told them that most poets were worth 'fuck-all' and at the moment he was working on a 'series of masturbatory poems which a man of his age can permit himself.' Paul was always linguistically inspired by sex: in *Parallèlement* he titled an erotic poem with the English word 'Auburn' because in French it could be read as '*aux burnes*', or 'to my bollocks'. His artist friend Cazals stated in *The*

Last Days of Paul Verlaine, 'Certain aberrations of sensual joy maintain a character of potency and virility, even joy, totally incompatible with modern neuroses', and advised readers to look behind the 'obscene rhymes' for 'infinite sadness' and 'a taste for humanity'. Cazals, whose visual obsession with the poet translated into dozens of drawings and etchings, was also his lover for a time, according to Alfred Vallette, director of *Mercure de France*.

Paul's ailments included rheumatism, cyrrhosis, gastritis, jaundice, diabetes, and cardiac hypertrophy. Memories also plagued him; he told Retté sadly, 'What weighs on me right now are not at all material worries – it's my dreams ... Since the death of Rimbaud, I see him every night.' He told Retté in a rasping voice, fixing his 'black diamond eyes' on him, 'I cannot accept this death. It's been some years now since we've seen each other, but Rimbaud, his art and his face, still shine in the back of my mind ... For me, Rimbaud is an ever-living reality, a sun that burns inside me that does not want to be put out ...That's why I dream of him every night.'

In his last years, Paul spent whatever royalties he earned on two middle-aged women prostitutes he lived with alternately. He also frequented a gay man, André Salis, nicknamed Bibi-la-Purée, an occasional thief. Robert Sherard, a friend and biographer of Oscar Wilde, explained that Bibi was notorious for stealing umbrellas: 'When he entered a café in the Latin Quarter or Montmartre, you saw everybody rushing for his *parapluie*.' Bibi's nickname was obscene, with *purée* a slang word for sperm. Still playing a double game, Paul would deny in print that his relationship to Arthur had been sexual while bragging about the truth to approving friends. One such, Retté, would later write, 'The only duty of poets is to confide to us sincerely the way they feel about life. If afterwards they neglect to put a fig leaf over their passions, that's their business.' Paul chided the critic Charles

Maurras's erotic interpretation of his praise of Arthur's 'matchless legs': 'Come now, Mr. Maurras, is your confusion between tirelessness and ... something else really in good faith?' In his *Confessions* and *Autobiographical Notes*, Paul denied any sexual relationship, but those he met knew otherwise. Paul, never as good a student as his lover, kept repeating the same errors as long as his strength lasted and, not coincidentally, kept writing. To stop writing would have meant that he had learnt his lesson and grown up. Biographers have dwelled on Paul's 'systematic destruction of his body' until his early death at age fifty-two, but longevity is in good part genetic and his son Georges, a respectable fellow, died at fifty-six, only four years older than his father. Paul outlived the Zutistes who mostly died in their forties or younger.

In 1896 Paul died in poverty. Compared to Arthur's lonely family funeral, his ceremony was a public event, with thousands of Parisians following the casket to the Batignolles cemetery. Admirers had pressed in to help in the final hours, such as Count Robert de Montesquiou, one of the models for Proust's Charlus; his lover and secretary Gabriel Yturri offended visitors by eating an orange and throwing the peels under the newly dead man's bed. Oscar Wilde told a story about the British journalist Rowland Strong who didn't deign to visit the dying man's squalid room and instead sent his butler, who reported imperturbably, 'I saw the gentleman, sir, and he died immediately.' Some critics like Petitfils have seen parallels between Oscar and Paul as homosexual writers who spent time in jail although the latter was not jailed for his homosexuality. On the occasions they had met, Oscar was put off by his shabbiness, shameless begging and self-indulgence, but praised him at a distance as 'the one Christian poet since Dante', saying that his was one of 'the two most perfect lives I have come across in my own experience', the other being that of the Russian Prince Kropotkin, who also spent time in jail. Oscar was drawn to his Christian conversion and claimed to hear a mystic version of Marsyas's cry in the suffering expressed in his poetry. In April 1895 during the Wilde trial the Belgian poet Georges Rodenbach said at the Goncourt home that pederasty was 'out of fashion' and that he planned to write an article on Paul, to which an editor shouted, 'No no, he slings his pederasty over his shoulder', implying that he used it like a rifle or other weapon.

Soon, however, their status as icons would develop in some quarters, at least. At the turn of the century, Paul Léautaud recalled that little plaster busts of Paul and Arthur had been placed on either side of a mantelpiece clock in the publisher's office at *Mercure de France*; they had become the mother and father of modern French letters, although it was unclear who was the mother and who the father. A first monument to Verlaine was raised in 1908 in Allauch, a small town near Marseilles, but Mathilde stated that a few days before the official unveiling 'miserable iconoclasts broke the monument', possibly a case of posthumous gay-bashing. Three years later the sculptor Rodo de Niederhausen's monument to Verlaine was raised in Paris's Luxembourg gardens, where it remains. A collection to build the monument had begun in 1897 and donors included poor schoolteachers, some able to give only twenty-five centimes. Havelock Ellis wrote about the statue, 'Amid roses and rhododenrons, nearby a Silenus in bronze rides among fauns, held up by naked nymphs. No spot in Paris could be more fittingly devoted to the memory of Verlaine, and here in autumn the mists that he loved and the purifying rain envelop him in their beneficent gloom.' But ironists still had their say: Wilde joked that the monument should have been placed in the Café François Premier, since 'the hero's statue must be on his life's battlefield.' And there was similar irony in William John Robertson's *A Century of French Verse* (1895), which dismissed Arthur as a talented failure with 'a certain bizarre fashion of looking at men and morals ... It is doubtful if Arthur Rimbaud could have conquered an important place in French literature, although with severe labour and discipline he might have produced some durable work.'

With V&R gone, there were more hauntings: Alfred Bardey refused to write a preface to a collection of Arthur's African letters as he didn't want to be haunted by him. Madame Rimbaud wrote to Isabelle in June 1899 that while praying at mass she saw 'Arthur himself: same height, age, face, grey-white skin, no beard but a small moustache, and missing a leg. The boy looked at me with extraordinary sympathy.' No doubt she relished this posthumous sympathy, because from her living son-in-law Paterne Berrichon, she received only insults in the preface to his 1899 volume of Arthur's letters: 'Her heart beats for money, and by tradition would not really respect a poor man, even if he were her son Arthur ... She believes herself a firm Catholic whereas she is nothing but an intolerant cleric who would have disdained Jesus.' Born Pierre Dufour, and afflicted with a bad stutter and lack of literary talent, he took an unconsciously comic pen name, meaning 'paternal figure from the Berry region.' A former supporter of the Commune who served time in jail, he became a fervent advocate of Isabelle's view of Arthur as a Catholic poet, rewriting his letters in order to make him seem a more successful businessman. Berrichon was so otiose that he inspired violent reaction and after each of his books, other writers hastened to correct him. His denials of Arthur's gayness became so strenuous that in March 1912 Rémy de Gourmont wrote in *Intimate Letters to the Amazon* addressed to the lesbian Nathalie Barney, that never before had there been accumulated so many 'proofs for the chastity of two friends who slept in the same bed.'

Madame Rimbaud boycotted a 1901 ceremony in which a bust of Arthur sculpted by Berrichon was unveiled on the Place de la Gare in Charleville. Discussing the poet's death in 1891, Paul Valéry had told Gide, 'In fifty years we'll build statues to him', but in fact it had only taken ten years. Frédéric, a busdriver in nearby Attigny, was there wearing an opera hat and frock coat. After 1905 Madame Rimbaud wore a sack at her waist containing money and IOUs. In 1907, the year of her death at age eighty-two, she wrote to Isabelle after hearing soldiers march by that she'd felt a strong emotion, 'in remembrance of your father with whom I would have been happy if I had not had certain children who made me suffer so much.'

Frédéric died in 1911 at age fifty-eight. He had married against his mother's wishes in 1885, and although he divorced ten years later, he was never forgiven and was refused burial in the family tomb. Frédéric had three children, all disowned by their aunt Isabelle. In response to Berrichon's books, Izambard published his memoirs in 1912. In the same year Berrichon produced an edition of the poems prefaced by Claudel that launched the myth of Rimbaud as good Catholic. In 1914 Mathilde Mauté, overweight and twice divorced, died at age sixty in Nice where she ran a family boarding house. That year Berrichon completed a second volume, *Jean-Arthur Rimbaud, le Voyageur* after much original research, especially in Africa. But a month before the 1918 Armistice, artillery fire destroyed the farm at Roche along with many documents and the only copy of his manuscript. Today a plaque adorns the ruins, noting that this is where *A Season in Hell* was written. Isabelle had died in 1917 at age fifty-seven of complications from cancer of the knee, the same illness that killed her brother. She underwent surgery, possibly a leg amputation at the American Hospital in Neuilly. Not until 1922 were her remains transferred to Charleville, while Berrichon noisily drank in a café near the cemetery. Three months later he died suddenly, after marrying his housemaid, 'in the best comic theatre tradition', as Etiemble noted. As the sole heir to the literary estate, the widow Marie Saulnier sold his papers to a book-dealer.

With Berrichon gone, Arthur's obscene works began to appear although not at *Mercure de France* where Claudel levied a ban: The Surrealists sponsored the first publication of *Les Stupra* in 1923 and in 1924 the anti-clerical satire *A Heart Under a Cassock*. The poet Louis Aragon, secretly homosexual before supporting Gay Liberation late in life, was instrumental in the publication of the anarchically sexual texts. In 1925 there appeared for the first time *What the Poet is Told About Flowers* which Marcel Coulon had found among the papers of Théodore de Banville. Pascal Pia edited an edition of *Les Stupra* under the pseudonym Marcelle La Pompe, which could be translated as Marcelle the Suction Pump. The next year the first reliable biography appeared by Jean-Marie Carré and Charleville celebrated the second unveiling of a bust. A previous statue had been removed and melted down for scrap during the First World War when the Germans occupied Charleville. The ceremony was interrupted by the distribution of a surrealist tract printed on blood-red paper, entitled, 'Excuse Me!' recalling Arthur's hatred for his hometown and predicting that the new bust 'will be sent back to us in the form of a shell', as the old one had. This did indeed happen, figuratively speaking. As part of the ceremony, some relics were displayed at Charleville, including Arthur's knife, fork, metal drinking cup, and perfume flask. These were lost before the Second World War when they were lent to an exhibition in Lille. The perfume flask is to be particularly regretted, otherwise a *parfumier* today might be able to market the scent of Rimbaud.

In 1930 Delahaye died at the age of seventy-seven and Izambard followed in 1931 at age eighty-three. Arthur's childhood had by now nearly escaped living memory except for a surviving friend, Paul Labarrière, who was hunted down at age seventy-eight and gave his recollections in the *Mercure de France* sixty-two years after the fact. Labarrière admitted that in 1885 he had lost a forty-page notebook of poetry entrusted to him and all he could remember were a few scraps of lines which are dutifully reproduced in collected editions. The final results of a royalty trial hit the newspapers in 1934 in which Frédéric's daughters, Nelly Lecourt and Emilie Tessier, sued Berrichon's widow, the total sales of Rimbaud's works by *Mercure de France* from 1898 to 1927 being worth 35,565.15 francs and the author's share 10,000 francs. The nieces first sued in 1928 and in 1930 the court decided against them because more than thirty years had elapsed between Rimbaud's death and their demand, and they lost again on appeal. The former housemaid continued to cash royalty checks, and in 1954, during her uncle's centennial, Madame Tessier stated on French television that she did not own a copy of his works since she received no royalties on them and therefore wouldn't buy one. The ghost of Madame Rimbaud has been as persistent in France as that of her son.

THE RIMBAUD STATUE IN CHARLEVILLE-MÉZIÈRE

Hauntings: from 1892 to today

In more than a century since Rimbaud's death some critics have lauded his work while deploring or misreading his life: this chapter will look at how his life and work, which are in fact inseparable, influenced other artists. The dominant influence has been Rimbaud's life, far greater than his work, which has generally been seen as a disastrous influence on too-slavish imitators. Yet to date most of the focus of Rimbaud studies has been on stylistic matters, whereas a wealth of documentation exists about how important he was personally to several generations of creative artists. Many of those discussed here, although by no means all, were gay. Rimbaud has been a licence to sexual freedom, and for making things new in any domain. Like all idols, he has also sometimes been seen as a restrictive obsession. The collective impression is of a continuity of reflection around Rimbaud, that argues forcefully for the concept of gay culture. For what else other than culture is this tradition of influence, maintained from generation to generation?

In 1893 the Spanish poet Rubén Darío described Verlaine in *Los raros*, a study of 'eccentric' writers: 'Rarely has a human brain been more violently and venemously bitten by the serpent of sex.' When Darío visited Verlaine at the Broussais Hospital he likened him to 'a figure painting by Ribera'. As for Rimbaud, Darío compared him to a noted Symbolist poet and art historian, finding him 'as bright as Georges Vanor among the geniuses, as great as Vanor but less confusing.' Darío's prestige was great and among those seduced by these descriptions was the poet Federico García Lorca, who at twenty in

May 1918, wrote a letter to a friend admitting his own gayness: 'I am a simple youth, passionate and silent, who almost, almost like the wonderful Verlaine, carries inside him a lily that cannot be watered and who presents to the imbecilic eye of those who look at him the image of a deep red rose with the sexual tinge of an April peony.'

Closer to the source was André Gide: In April 1912, Gide received from Claudel two photos of Arthur reproduced from originals in the Berrichon collection. Gide soon criticized Claudel for ignoring 'the ferocious side of Rimbaud's personality ... and his relations with Verlaine.' In March 1914, Claudel detected what he called a 'pederastic passage' in an excerpt by Gide in the *Nouvelle revue française* and asked in a letter to its editor, 'Is that why he so desires to see the same morals attributed to Arthur Rimbaud, and doubtless to Whitman?' In a 1947 interview, Claudel preferred not to speak of Rimbaud, who had been so 'prostituted' and whose work had been 'soiled': 'It's like a lovely artistic place one has just discovered, and soon one finds garbage and sardine cans there. You can't go there any more.'

Another contemporary, Marcel Proust, would appreciate him all the more for the so-called 'soiled' aspects, writing to a friend in April, 1918 that 'morally pure' artists were 'academic dried fruits who are no use to anyone, while by contrast the new word which uncovers a still-unknown parcel of the mind, a supplementary nuance of tenderness, spurts out of the drunkenness of a Musset or Verlaine, the perversions of a Baudelaire or Rimbaud or a Wagner, the epilepsy of a Flaubert.' Yet to Proust some perversions could seem divine. In January 1920 he wrote to the author Jacques Rivière that Rimbaud was 'a case that was particular, extraordinary, almost extra-human.'

Jean Cocteau said as much when he assimilated Arthur to his private mythology, 'a mixture of Ganymede and the eagle, an angel brutal in eternity.' From 1917, when Cocteau wrote a poem in homage to Arthur, until 1963, when one of his last works was a prose essay in homage to the poet, Cocteau's life and work were obsessed with Rimbaud, whom he saw both as a father and son. He described a series of adolescent lovers, many of whom died young, as versions of Rimbaud, and even the French mathematician Evariste Galois who died in a duel at twenty-one in 1832 was pitied by Cocteau because he 'didn't even have his Verlaine'. He conferred Rimbaud's mantle on other gay writers such as the novelist and thief Jean Genet, on trial in July 1943. He wrote that Genet 'steals to nourish his body and soul. He's Rimbaud, and we can't convict Rimbaud.' A defence lawyer read out the letter and Genet was acquitted. The French fascist newspaper *Je suis partout* stated that Genet 'takes himself for Villon because of his criminal record and for Rimbaud because of his chosen morality.'

Like Gide, Cocteau displayed a copy of the Carjat portrait in his home, and wrote that the faded photograph was 'a sort of miracle ... His lower lip, in reality heavy, vanishes. He seems to bite it. His eyes are stars. One might say an angel, a materialization.' In 1921 Cocteau agreed to organize events for the nightclub *le Boeuf sur le toit* because its owner, Louis Moysès, a gay man who grew up in Charleville, had once lived in Arthur's former family home. In *The Difficulty of Being*, he wrote, 'What makes France great? Villon, Rimbaud, Verlaine, Baudelaire.' Cocteau hoped that this greatness would force a wider acceptance of homosexuality: 'One could fear that the storms of the Verlaine-Rimbaud couple might shock Glory who is a woman. Yet once again morality must bow before genius, for genius is only the phenomenon that consists of sanctifying painted, written, or lived mistakes.' He added, 'If I don't speak of Marseilles in 1891, it's that this period is intolerable for me – I suffer all its pains ... we must see in the amputation a proof of the combat with the angel and the ferocious love of the Muses, like that of the Praying Mantis devouring its husband.' He believed that Arthur drew his fate upon himself, that he 'realized too late that the Muses are ladies you don't turn your back on and if you disdain them, they get their revenge and make you pay very dearly.' Although 'poets owe everything' to him, Cocteau wrote in an open letter to Jacques Maritain in 1926, that Arthur was 'at the moment more of a burden' for writers than Victor Hugo.

This was also the complaint of another French poet, Max Jacob. For a brief time apparently the lover of the surrealist writer Michel Leiris, Jacob wrote to a friend in October 1923 about Arthur's influence:

> *I am worried about young Leiris … I wanted him to have wings, and he's a duck – let him fly! He drags his feet. Let's not say anything bad about Rimbaud, that brings bad luck, but why not, why not be the Rimbaud of 1923. It's so easy! Tell him to walk three times a week in the East of Paris, to eat with the poor one day and with dukes the next, not to think of literature but let it think of him. He thinks about Rimbaud, good god! The way to think of him is to forget him completely. That sparrow-hawk will know how to catch up with him.*

Jacob wrote to the author Marcel Jouhandeau about another friend in September 1925: 'Rimbaud is spoiling his literary taste. Who will get rid of Rimbaud for us? You!' He complained about young writers' unoriginality: 'When they have nothing to say, they say 'Rimbaud' all day long, their beaks in a dictionary.' Yet he informed Jouhandeau, 'A powerful education is absolutely necessary for a writer. Rimbaud had it. He won all the prizes in his collège and I've got very precise information about it from the organist at Charleroi who was his relative.' Jacob, who had discovered many talented adolescents, including Radiguet, wrote in a joking letter to a friend in May 1937 that Goffin's 'Rimbaud Vivant', offered 'the key to *Illuminations* and that key is a phallus which is like Columbus' egg whereby everything is explained and worked out: At last I'll be able to read Rimbaud with something to understand.'

By the 1920s other gay creators had assimilated the poet into their daily lives, among them René Crevel, the only openly gay Surrealist. In an August 1926 note to Jouhandeau, Crevel compared his affair with a Kansas City-born pianist, Eugene MacCown, nicknamed Coconotte or Eugénie, with the tumultuous V&R couple. The gay American poet Hart Crane used a line by Arthur as an epigraph to his poem 'The Bridge' and cited him in letters as a guide to gay lifestyle as well as poetry. In 1920 Crane stated in a letter to a friend about Washington, DC: 'Every other person in the government service and diplomatic service are enlarged editions of Lord Douglas. Amusing Household! as Rimbaud would say.' In 1927 he reported to a friend from Hollywood, 'Just walk down Hollywood Boulevard someday – if you must have something out of uniform. Here are little fairies who can quote Rimbaud before they are 18.' Crane wrote to Waldo Frank in 1926, 'Rimbaud was the last great poet that our civilization will see – he let off all the great cannon crackers in Valhalla's parapets, the sun has set theatrically several times since, while Laforgue, Eliot, and others of that kidney have whimpered fastidiously.'

For Crane, Arthur was a reminder of the savage essence of poetry, and the danger for gay writers of settling into a comfortable existence. Gide had a similar notion when he wrote in his *Journal*, 'Reading Rimbaud or the sixth *Song of Maldoror* makes me ashamed of my works, and disgusted at all that's merely a result of culture.' The lesbian writer Marguerite Yourcenar, author of the *Memoirs of Hadrian*, identified her father, Michel René de Crayencour, with Arthur despite a lack of physical resemblance. She told an interviewer that the two men were near-contemporaries of 'robust country origin ... the aspect of the man with shoe-soles of wind, at home anywhere and nowhere, a taste for life and an almost total lack of looking at the past (one doesn't get the impression that Rimbaud thought much about his poems, his brief and brilliant career in poetry, once it ended) and finally, a supreme and instinctive disdain for current opinions and prejudices which made them, through the highs and lows of their lives, free men.'

By the 1930s Arthur was an inextricable myth in French gay life. The 1939 novel by Jean-Paul Sartre, *The Wall* discussed him as a gay icon: a high-school student, Lucien, is seduced by a friend, Bergère, who refers to the poem 'The Seated Ones' to justify himself – 'It's a hideous, deliberate error of the 'Seated Ones' to believe that there are exclusive objects of sexual desire, namely women, because they have a hole between their legs.' He tells Lucien, 'You are Rimbaud. He had your large hands. When he came to Paris to see Verlaine he had your pink face of a healthy young countryman and the long slender body of a blonde young girl.' Lucien was shocked to be lent a copy of *Illuminations* because 'Rimbaud was a pederast', but soon looked in the mirror and repeated, 'I'm Rimbaud,' while his friend joked, 'You're counting on me to disorder all your little senses ... Damn little bluffer, wants to play Rimbaud but after more than an hour I still haven't managed to excite him.'

A pendant to Goffin's book celebrating Arthur's homosexuality was the diatribe of a gallic Colonel Blimp whose first name has been lost to posterity and in bibliographies he is known only as 'Colonel Godchot'. In *Rimbaud Ne Varietur* he described Paul as 'a disgusting pederast' and quivered with rage at 'the excuses found for these infamous morals, these scenes of sodomy, these pederastic vices in which the two poets soiled themselves.' From an opposite point of view to Goffin's, Godchot also claimed that V&R's sexuality pervaded their work: 'Their poems and prose have thrown the horrors of their morals to the universe.' Yet Godchot did make some important contributions and his verve made the subject of V&R's gayness that much more difficult to avoid. A more sympathetic interpretation was offered in a play by Maurice Rostand, *Verlaine*, which opened in 1939 in Paris. The son of Edmond Rostand, author of *Cyrano de Bergerac,* Maurice was one of the most conspicuous gay men in the Paris arts world, who curled his hair and dyed it blond to better resemble Sarah Bernhardt, and wore jackets with little epaulettes, looking, as one witness put it, 'like a fat lady playing a bellhop in a revue'. Rostand would receive visitors in his Paris apartment while casting longing glances out his window at a *pissotière* located just below, convenient for trysts. Rostand's play, one of a series of dramas in defence of Wilde and other gays, was reviewed sarcastically by Petitfils who called it 'weak, lachrymose, full of errors', adding, 'we can guess – alas! – the motive why the author of *The Woman Inside Him* chose as main plot the painful Verlaine-Rimbaud affair.'

In Britain George Moore's feeble myths were not the last word on the matter, as Bloomsbury had also discovered the poet: Lytton Strachey's *Eminent Victorians* (1918) did not mention General Gordon's homosexuality, but by citing Arthur as another Sudan dweller – who referred to Gordon as an 'idiot' in an 1885 letter – he implicitly raised the subject: 'The amazing poet of the *Saison d'Enfer* (sic) amid those futile turmoils of petty commerce in which, with an inexplicable deliberation, he had forgotten the enchantments of an unparalleled adolescence, forgotten the fogs of London and the streets of Brussels, forgotten Paris, forgotten the subtleties and the frenzies of inspiration, forgotten the agonized embraces of Verlaine.' By contrast, another Bloomsbury product, *The Apology of Arthur Rimbaud: a Dialogue* by Edward Sackville-West, published in 1927 by Leonard and Virginia Woolf's Hogarth Press, denied any sexual relationship with Paul in an imaginary dialogue with the dead Arthur, presumably because the generation of British gays after the Wilde trial felt that any V&R sexual affair would be a defamation of the adored youth.

By comparison, Enid Starkie's 1937 *Rimbaud in Abyssinia* and 1938 biography, were exuberantly frank yet tolerant, as unflappable as the modestly titled *Sketch for a Portrait of Rimbaud* by Humphrey Hare, which also appeared in London in 1937. Starkie's own unhappiness with heterosexuality and her crypto-lesbian friendships may have made her less judgmental than other writers and her spirit was like an intellectual version of Coward's Madame Arcati skimming over the hills of Oxford on her bicycle. Starkie wrote, 'It is impossible to prove conclusively whether Verlaine and Rimbaud actually practiced sodomy', but ended the same paragraph thus: 'if the poems written by Verlaine are taken as further evidence, little doubt can remain in a reasonable reader's mind that sodomy must indeed have been practised.' She never lost sight of the pleasure principle: 'Of the physical rapture felt by both the men no doubt can be entertained ...' and of their mutual inspiration, she noted, 'It was during the time of the height of his passion for Verlaine that he produced the largest part of his work and this period coincided with his belief in himself and in his doctrine of art.' She also offered personal insights into the potential pain of same-sex relationships: 'Only two members of the same sex have power to wound one another so deeply when things go wrong between them, and to wound one another where hurt is most intolerable.'

One of Starkie's many admiring readers was Wystan Auden, who wrote a sonnet in December 1938, 'Rimbaud', not one of his best because of its flat rhymes and false premises: Arthur's 'horrible companions did not know it' but the 'cold had made a poet'. In fact, they knew well that he was a gifted poet. However, Auden introduced Benjamin Britten to the poetry and the result was 'Les Illuminations' for vocal soloist (preferably soprano) and string orchestra. Britten set music to 'Antique', about a hermaphrodite statue and dedicated it to a boy he loved, Wulf Scherchen. Among the other prose poems set were 'Royalty', in which a loving couple consider themselves to be king and queen, the triumphant seascape 'Marine', and the erotic 'I alone possess the key', dedicated to his lover Peter Pears who sang the premiere of the work. His dedications were coded initials, 'KHWS' for Scherchen and 'PNLP' for Pears, who later explained that to Britten, Arthur was one of those 'bewildered but gifted young of whom he was fond: "lost sheep" as he called them.' The composer discreetly omitted a line from the poem 'Parade', about 'taking it from behind'. Like Proust or Lorca, Britten was an often disapproving moralist about gay matters and made these settings as he did others to texts by Michelangelo, Mann, Melville, Forster, and Owen, partly to explore gay cultural identity.

One friend who listened was the choreographer Frederick Ashton, who created a memorable ballet to Britten's score. Ashton had been acquainted with the poems since 1941 and said that he 'used to weep when I read about him', which was probably in Enid Starkie's books. The choreographer first heard 'Les Illuminations' in 1945, however, he abandoned the theme temporarily because he considered it as being 'too risqué for the English'. He finally did choreograph the work as a portrait of V&R's stay in London, inspired by a lover named Dick Beard who stated that Ashton 'saw a lot of Rimbaud and Verlaine in the two of us, or concerned himself poetically with the idea.' In the ballet Arthur flings confetti: as the biographer Julie Kavanagh wrote, 'an image of falling stars and an emblem of ejaculation, enacting a line from one of Ashton's love letters to Beard: "How can I forget when you showered me with stars." ' In the 'Being Beauteous' section Ashton incorporated a black dancer as a reference to Rimbaud's beloved Abyssinian companion, Djami Wadaï, and there was a scene of zipping up flies outside a public urinal which offended London audiences in 1947. However, the ballet marked an appropriation of V&R's story by gay creators on the international scene. Other postwar gay composers have made settings, including Hans Werner Henze, whose 'Being Beauteous' from 1963 set a section from *Illuminations*. The work for coloratura soprano, harp, and four cellos was inspired by a late-night visit to New York City's Harlem where Henze felt a mixture of 'sweetness and fear, dissolution and danger' that reminded him of the poet.

It is curious that in France there was less ardent acceptance of Arthur's life and work as a unity. The Catholic writer François Mauriac, who was a closeted gay, paraphrased in his *Bloc-Notes* the phrase 'strange and sad error' from *A Season in Hell* to refer to homosexuality. A political arch-conservative, Mauriac wrote, 'As Rimbaud said of love, the right wing in France must be reinvented.' He certainly adored the 'soiled adolescent who threw a piercing scream toward lost purity' in *A Season in Hell* but described Claudel's play *Golden Head* with its friendship between adolescent boys as 'a love in which sex plays no part', adding that 'Claudel was thinking of Rimbaud, the Rimbaud we prefer to the one who had the "mysterious delicacies."' The delicacies in question, meaning gay sex, were also a paraphrase from *A Season in Hell*. For Mauriac it was extremely difficult having such 'madmen' as literary masters as 'each cry in Rimbaud responds to what I myself have suffered.'

Less self-identification and more sexual desire was the response of Marcel Jouhandeau who published literary diaries, *Journaliers*, in which he described his love affairs with men and how his wife Elise disapproved of them. In 1967 Elise read to him from the biography by Pierre Arnoult which was published in 1943 in Occupied Paris. Jouhandeau was fascinated to hear his wife reading the passage that detailed the supposed rape by Communards with the imagined dialogue, 'Strip, kid!' and details like 'Rimbaud was on the ground, knocked over.' Jouhandeau declared that through this rape he 'acquired a new dimension forever. He carries within himself in his body the experience of abjection.' Despite Elise's preaching, Jouhandeau was attracted to him – he wrote that in a Paris park in 1961 he had observed 'a chérubin, a bit thuggish, as disturbing and distinguished as the young Rimbaud, whose photograph we own.' The Carjat photo was displayed as an erotic talisman *chez* Jouhandeau as it was in the homes of Cocteau and Gide.

In Germany as in France, Arthur attracted creative artists: the circle of gay poets around Stefan George admired the latter's translations of poems by V&R as early as 1905. But George did not approve of their lives, telling a friend in 1927 that Paul's *Notes On My Life* were 'still under the signpost marked swinishness (*cochonnerie*) in literature.' The novelist Stefan Zweig produced a short book on Verlaine which was translated into English in 1913. Zweig's Rimbaud was ...

> ... *a big robust fellow with a demonic physical force like that which Balzac breathed into his Vautrin types. He was a provincial with massive red fists and the curious face of a child that has been corrupted early in life ... everything in him is force, over-abundant, wild, exceptional virility ... He is one of the conquistador types, who first lost his way in literature ... Like a crater he throws out his mad fever dreams and visions of life such as perhaps only Dante has had before him.*

Zweig granted that 'without doubt there was an element of the abnormal' in V&R's relations, but stated that 'it is not necessary nor essential to know whether the dangerous potentialities that inhere in so strong a personal enthusiasm ever became material facts.' Zweig admired *Femmes/Hombres* but was troubled by its 'unheard-of subjective shamelessness. In form the poems are smooth and in structure they are clever. But ... they are naked and obscene. The effect of this depravity of an old man writing down with unsteady hand vices and nakednesses on prescription blanks for the sake of a few francs with which to buy an absinthe, is tragic.'

The 'shamelessness' attracted a later generation of German writers, notably Bertolt Brecht. His biographer John Fuegi has described Brecht's bisexuality, for many years 'attracted to both sexes for sex, but he really preferred the company of men.' One friend recalled that Brecht appreciated 'dandified men of the ... Rimbaud type', meaning that he liked adolescents, since Arthur was not really a dandy. Brecht's early plays *Baal* and *In the Jungle of Cities* are both influenced by the V&R couple, quoting their poetry in translation without attribution and staging their violent homoerotic relationship, influenced by Zweig's account. The character Baal was a 'bisexual poet-singer-murderer'. *In the Jungle of Cities*, set in a mythical Chicago, tells of a sadomasochistic love relationship between two men. One character, Garga, has a speech which is taken almost word-for-word from *Season in Hell*, in the translation by K.L. Ammer published in Leipzig in 1907. This Brecht cheerfully admitted in his diary for October 1921: 'I'm skimming through the Rimbaud volume and doing some borrowing. How incandescent the whole thing is! Shining paper! And his shoulders are made of bronze ...'

By contrast, the novelist Thomas Mann, whose homosexuality the biographer Anthony Heilbut has explored, complained in 1939 that 'the greatly gifted Rimbaud' had 'demolished' moral strictures in France. Mann's son Klaus told his friend Stefan Zweig in June 1934 that he wanted to write a book on his 'old and strong love, Rimbaud'. Klaus wrote in his diary on May 12 of the same year: 'Work as salvation. Desire to begin a large RIMBAUD.' In 1939 he noted in his journal his aim to write a series of 'tragic-grotesque artist novellas' with gay themes among them, such as V&R, Nijinsky's madness, and Wilde in Paris. Unfortunately he never wrote the book.

In Germany the legacy was thus seen as tragic, but in Italy ever since Vittorio Pica's *Letteratura d'eccezione* (1898) called Arthur a 'bizarre and precocious homosexual', Italian gays have taken him as inspiration. In 1937, at age fifteen the poet and director Pier Paolo Pasolini heard 'The Drunken Boat' read aloud in his *liceo* class. For Pasolini this was a 'literary and political baptism that swept away academic and provincial culture, Fascist conformity, and put the social identity itself of the young poet into question,' according to his biographer Nico Naldini. Pasolini soon saw himself as a 'Rimbaud without the talent' as he joked to friends, an empowered gay adolescent. He wrote to a friend in 1948 at age twenty-five that he had 'satisfied certain terrific (sexual) needs of adolescence and of first youth. I feel like trying again to give myself illusions and desires once more; I am definitely a little Villon or a little Rimbaud.' Pasolini was prepared to embark on travels to search for an inspiring lover: to Guatemala or even to Paris, he claimed.

The director Luchino Visconti also identified with him. In the summer of 1947, Visconti surprised friends by leaving Rome for adventure in Sicily, quoting from 'The Drunken Boat' in a letter to explain his decision: 'Adventure is a prelude to other griefs, other things, especially other struggles. "And the stains of blue wine and of vomit — I wash off."' Identifying new explorations of the heart with artistic adventures, Italians such as Pasolini and Visconti embodied a unified and coherent transmission of the poet's life and art. Another example, the poet Sandro Penna, wrote a brief revery, 'Literature': 'Evening in July, across the river,/ song of drunken boys./ On a bench, a shadowed void. / Once I was Hölderlin ... Rimbaud.'

In 1949 in Paris a storm of publicity broke over a forged prose poem, supposedly the lost 'Spiritual Hunt', fabricated by a theatre director, Nicholas Bataille, and a woman colleague, Akakia-Viala. Bataille was irked when his 1948 staged version of *Season in Hell* was panned by critics who hated the concept. Critics had been complaining about the suitability of staged versions of *A Season in Hell* since the first one by Paul Fort's Théâtre de l'Art in 1890. To prove they knew more than the critics, Bataille and Akakia-Viala wrote a five-part prose poem and claimed they had discovered a lost work by Rimbaud. Its headings were Vaudeville, Pagan Vacations, Edens, Infirmities, and Swamps, followed by a sixth, Bastard Loves, after the fraud was admitted. Bataille's 'Spiritual Hunt' was a glum, drab exercise, but some literary lions such as Mauriac were fooled. Others denounced it as a fake, amongst them Breton and Cocteau, finding it 'laborious and soul-less'. Just back from a tour to Egypt when the scandal broke, Cocteau added how delightful it was to be back in Paris where all anyone talked about was a poem. To prove they had faked it, Bataille and Akakia-Viala wrote a sixth chapter, 'Bastard Loves', as an 'inversion' of the Foolish Virgin's monologue in *Season in Hell*, in which Arthur spoke about Paul: 'Stories of irresistible sabbaths where fallen angels clung to one another, handsomer than assassins ... To surprise him, I cultivated gestures of affection, inventing for myself alone dances of tragic daggers. He watched me sleep. With the graces of Mary, with repented kindnesses, he crowned the elegance of our vices ... We had caressed the sin with new hands, clumsy and trembling with mysterious questions.' The forgers produced an overtly gay segment after their imposture was revealed, making it the only part written as a blatant fake that dared speak its name.

While France was preoccupied with this imposture, in America at the beginning of the McCarthy era a play about V&R was staged off-Broadway. *A Season in Hell*, by the Greek-born Jewish writer and translator of Cavafy, Rae Dalven, unfortunately remained unpublished. Another reaction to America's political conservativism was the Beat literary movement. The gay Beats led by Allen Ginsberg admired Rimbaud for his experiments with drugs, alcohol, and sex. Ginsberg explained to students at Kent State University:

> *I kept thinking I was in love with Kerouac and I also was in love with somebody*
> *else, another cat who looked exactly like Rimbaud, who actually looks like about half*
> *the people in this room at this point. So I immediately transferred the same erotic*
> schwärmerei, *the same erotic pleasure, to Rimbaud and then I fell in love with*
> *Rimbaud's writing because it was the manifestation of his seed, so to speak – I felt I*
> *could get inside his body through his writing 'cause I saw a photo of Rimbaud ...*

Kerouac, a bisexual himself, explained a love affair with a male junior high school classmate by saying that every Rimbaud needs a Verlaine (*New York Times*, July 9, 1998). A spiritual heir to Ginsberg's vision was the Algerian poet Jean Sénac. He was politically active, and found young Algerian revolutionaries sexually and artistically inspiring, but he was assassinated in 1973 at the age of forty-seven. His poem to one of revolutionaries, 'Ordres II', dated October 1970, stated: 'When I will have retired my poet/ my faggot my beard my bastard/ my algerian my sleep/ amid the vigorous tenderness of morning/ (knee intact, Rimbaud saved)/ You'll love me.' Unlike Sénac's revolutionary view, there were some French artists in the 1970s and 1980s who made the poet into a poster-boy, a familiar decal. The painter Ernest Pignon Ernest reproduced sweetened images based on the Carjat photo upon walls all over Paris where the banality of mechanical repetition matched the inspidity of the pretty, mournful Pierrot face. In a vital response, David Wojnarowicz, an American writer, photographer, and later an AIDS activist, produced a 1978–79 series of photographs, 'Rimbaud in New York', showing a young man wearing an insipid Carjat-inspired mask in a series of poses: on the subway, at a diner, and in bed with his pants and shirt open, holding his erect cock in his hand. Arthur-as-sad-Pierrot was given back his gender, forcefully.

'MUSIC SWEETENS THE MORALS' BY VERLAINE

In the 1970s various rock stars continued to be inspired by the poet. A leading example was Jim Morrison of the Doors. The emeritus professor and translator Wallace Fowlie was motivated by Morrison's life to write *Rimbaud and Jim Morrison*, but the book did not truly bring the two together, in part because Fowlie never discussed Morrison's bisexuality. Morrison's taste influenced the American screenwriter John Milius who explained in an interview that he had named the screen character 'Rambo', played by Sylvester Stallone, after the French poet loved by the rockstar. Yet dozens of headline writers later punned about the similarity in sound between 'Rambo' and 'Rimbaud' as if it were a coincidence they had just discovered instead of a deliberate invention by Milius.

By the 1980s punk rockers such as Patti Smith and guitarist Tom Verlaine were inspired by the poet's violence, obscenity, drugs, drink, and sexual unconventionality. Rocker Michael Stipe recalled going on a pilgrimage with Smith to the old building in Marseilles where Rimbaud died but they were disappointed to find 'a modern hospital' in its place. Such touristic pilgrimages became institutionalized during the centenary of his death in 1991. The French Cultural Ministry celebrated with a marathon foot-race from the Ardennes to Paris's Parc de la Villette, where an all-night party was held. Fifty fax machines in the park printed the poems in translation sent from French embassies around the world. The Minister of Culture started a chain letter of poems by sending one to the Prime Minister and a 'drunken boat' of French 'poets and actors' was chartered to retrace his travels in Africa and the Middle East. *La Quinzaine littéraire* headlined the celebrations 'Rimbaud Disgraced!' The poet's gayness was hardly mentioned in official circles, but *Globe* magazine conducted a poll which showed that some thirty-five per cent of French schoolchildren knew that Rimbaud had had a homosexual relationship but thought it was with Victor Hugo.

In contrast to the French activities, in Turin the author and puppeteer Guido Ceronetti staged 'Travel, Travel Rimbaud!', an 'ideophoric' marionette show. He explained that ideophoric marionettes had ...

> *... nothing to do with the tradition of popular marionettes that tell stories – they just appear, suggest, and disappear, not, however, without leaving a trace in the spectator's mind like a little invisible burn that no one feels just at that moment, and the feeling of having participated in a ceremony of initiation celebrated by*

chance and not expected by the puppeteers themselves. One may approach Arthur Rimbaud and especially the Rimbaud of extreme visions by such modes of expression, where the marionettes too have 'shoe-soles of wind'. It's not about the story of his life or an account of his travels but an alternation of symbolic prologues and evocations of a forgotten life, ideal flashes across which a poet wandering in time like Rimbaud might recognize (while denying them) his own disarming deliria.

Ceronetti, one of the few real poets to speak up during the centenary, called his show a 'light magic spider's web, an enigmatic yet fraternal faery play'.

After the centenary Rimbaud's fame continued to increase: Rudolf Nureyev, who died of AIDS in January 1993, asked for the poem 'Genius' to be read at his memorial ceremony in Paris's Palais Garnier. Agnieszka Holland's 1995 film, *Total Eclipse*, based on Christopher Hampton's play, focused on misbehaviour to the point of alienating spectators. *The New York Times*, interviewing the actor who played Arthur, Leonardo di Caprio, announced that the poet was 'utterly untutored in his art' and was known to 'urinate on guests at a dinner party', new inventions for the myth. Reviewing the film, London's *Guardian* admitted that V&R were 'pretty talented poets' but spoke of Di Caprio's 'nasty if pretty little prick of a Rimbaud', while Verlaine was 'so boorish that you can't believe he ever wrote anything halfway decent.' The gifted di Caprio was plausible but David Thewlis, the actor playing Paul, towered over him like a praying mantis, falsifying their real physical rapport. Hampton changed a number of details of the love affair, notably around the shooting incident, which made a murky mix of truth and fiction.

Also in 1995, Marcel Marceau likened Michael Jackson, then under fire for alleged pedophilia, to V&R. The occasion was a television programme in which the French mime worked with Jackson, stating that he was 'in the tradition of Verlaine and Rimbaud because his subject is the lost childhood'. When Eric Cantona retired, it was mentioned in the press that the footballer 'admired rebels: the painter Nicholas de Staël, the actor Mickey Rourke, the poet Rimbaud.' Rock musicians have appropriated the names, as well as the poetry: Robin Rimbaud leads the group Scanner, mixing electronic music with gatherings of information from the airwaves. Jim Carroll, author of *The Basketball Diaries*, Bob Dylan, and Lou Reed are all frequently compared to Rimbaud by journalists.

His 'matchless legs' have also inspired ballets: Choregrapher Peter Reed made a 'biography in dance' of Arthur entitled *Absent Moon*, following a ballet choreographed by John Butler, *A Season in Hell* (1967) to music by Peggy Glanville-Hicks. Butler had dancers representing V&R and 'The Woman' or Muse, which led *The New Yorker* to wisecrack that 'the trouble with poets is that they never get the girl'. Composer Kevin Volan's opera *The Man Who Strides the Wind*, inspired by his life was premiered in 1993, but years before, John Tavener's opera *Thérèse* (1976) had intertwined the contemporaneous lives of Saint Thérèse of Lisieux and Arthur to better effect. A *New York Times* humour column in March 1996 listed celebrity couples with V&R named alongside Beavis and Butthead, Divine Brown and Hugh Grant, Mick Jagger and Keith Richard, and in 1997 Arthur was included in Andrew Harvey's anthology of *Essential Gay Mystics*. About the future, Etiemble wrote, 'All Gods are mortal, and Rimbaud is God. Therefore Rimbaud is mortal.' Nevertheless Arthur and Paul look likely to remain the most celebrated gay couple in literary history.

The number of gay creators who have taken Rimbaud's life and art to their hearts is impressive. More than just his youth and beauty, they have also admired his brilliance, energy, and immense poetic will. And this will, and his life story, have impressed others as much as the actual words he wrote, always prey to the dilution of translations, and indeed often enigmatic in the original. Any number of Rimbaud's most ardent admirers have only a vague idea of his actual poems, but a crystal clear interpretation of his life and persona. In this sense as Etiemble stated many times, Rimbaud will always transcend literature and dwell in the domain of myth. Overturning idols and breaking all the rules is never done without consequences. Rimbaud's acceptance of these consequences further allies him to gay people, whose public self-definition usually requires an attitude of courageous openness and damn the consequences. Rimbaud's self-acceptance as *maudit* is another kind of model.

At a time when past gay rights legislation is repealed and new anti-gay laws are put on the books in America and Britain, prejudice can sometimes seem to supplant understanding. As we have seen, a number of V&R's friends and contemporaries proved unshockably sympathetic to their lifestyle and acts, whereas some people today are still offended by them. In this respect the 'politically correct' movement has achieved little so far for the rights of gays. Among minority studies programs in universities, gay studies departments are still generally poor cousins. And in the past two decades the attempt at general mobilization against the devastation of AIDS has so far gained only partial, belated results. The ideals of the ACT-UP organization are an echo of Rimbaud's revolutionary credos and violent militancy, courageously unheeding of conventions.

So, although Rimbaud has inspired many people in the past, his influence is even more urgently needed as we enter a new century.

Bibliography and suggested reading

Wallace Fowlie's translation of the poems, printed with the French (University of Chicago Press) is preferable to the Penguin translation by Olivier Bernard of 1962, which is marred by errors and an outdated preface. Paul Schmidt's inexact translation does not include the French original. Readers of French will enjoy the three paperbacks of Rimbaud's *Oeuvres* edited by Jean-Luc Steinmetz in the Garnier-Flammarion series. Other reliable texts are André Guyaux's Classiques Garnier volume, Cecil Hackett's for the Imprimerie nationale, and Louis Forestier's in the Laffont Bouquins series. Although outdated in some respects, the Gallimard Pléiade text, edited by Antoine Adam, contains a vast correspondence from the African years. Buyers should beware the faulty edition organized by Alain Borer for Arléa.

Among biographies of Rimbaud, Enid Starkie's is still valuable although some theories have been proven wrong and minor errors left uncorrected. Pierre Petitfils' book, which has been translated, offers better sources than interpretation; the more up-to-date and complete effort by Jean-Luc Steinmetz merits translation as does a recent life of Verlaine by Alain Buisine. In English, Lawrence and Elisabeth Hanson's 1958 book offers a tolerant view of Verlaine, whose poetry is best read in the original, for example in Jacques Robichez's Classiques Garnier edition, and the same is true of his erotica, all translations being inexact. Michael Pakenham's announced edition of Verlaine's correspondence will be a major event.

What follows here is a highly selective bibliography used for the present study. Readers of French may want to subscribe to *Parade Sauvage*, the Rimbaud studies magazine, and *Revue Verlaine*. At the time of going to press the former costs 170 francs for foreign subscribers and the latter 160 francs: checks are payable to the order of 'Monsieur le Receveur de Charleville-Mézières'; send to: Musée Rimbaud, BP 490 F-08109 Charleville-Mézières cedex FRANCE.

The Rimbaud Museum is at Le Vieux Moulin, quai Arthur Rimbaud, F-08000 Charleville-Mézières, Ardennes, France. Phone: (33) 24.33.31.64. Open every day except Monday from 10am to 12 noon and from 2pm to 6pm except national holidays.

Selected bibliography

On Rimbaud

Berrichon, Paterne and Rimbaud, Jean-Arthur, *Le Poète (1854–1873)*,
    Mercure de France, Paris, 1912

Bivort, Olivier and Murphy, Steve, *Rimbaud, Publications autour d'un centenaire,*
    Rosenberg & Sellier, Torino, 1994

Bonnefoy, Yves, *Rimbaud*, Seuil, Paris, 1961

Borer, Alain, 'De Arturi Rimbaldi latinis carminibus', in *Europe–revue littéraire,*
    June- July 1991

Bourgignon, Jean and Houin, Charles, *La Vie d'Arthur Rimbaud,*
    Payot, Paris, 1991 (reprint)

Bouchor, Maurice, *Les Chansons joyeuses*, Paris, 1874

Briet, Suzanne, *Rimbaud Notre Prochain,* Nouvelles éditions latines, Paris, 1956
    Madame Rimbaud, Les Lettres modernes, 1968
    (ed.) *Exposition Rimbaud,* Bibliothèque nationale, Paris, 1954

Breton, André, *Flagrant délit,* Thésée, Paris, 1949

Carré, Jean-Marie, *La Vie aventureuse de Jean-Arthur Rimbaud,* Plon, Paris, 1926

Cendo, Nicolas, *Arthur Rimbaud et les artistes du XXième siècle*, Musées de Marseille, 1991

Coulon, Marcel, *Le Problème de Rimbaud, poète maudit,* A. Gomès, Nîmes, 1923
    Au coeur de Verlaine et de Rimbaud, Le Livre, Paris, 1925
    Raoul Ponchon, Grasset, Paris, 1927

La Vie de Rimbaud et de son oeuvre, Mercure de France, Paris, 1929

Darío, Rubén, *Obras Completas,* tomo II, Biblioteca Rubén Darío, Madrid, 1950

Daulté, François, *Jean-Louis Forain,* la Bibliothèque des arts, Paris, 1995

Delahaye, Ernest, *Rimbaud, l'artiste et l'être moral,* Messein, Paris, 1923

   Souvenirs familiers à propos de Rimbaud, Verlaine, et Nouveau, Messein, Paris, 1925

   Les Illuminations et Une Saison en Enfer, Messein, Paris, 1927

   Delahaye témoin de Rimbaud, La Baconnière, Paris, 1974

Druick, Douglas, *Fantin-Latour,* The Gallery for the Corporation of the National
   Museums of Canada, Ottawa, 1983

Dufour, Hélène and Guyaux, André (eds), *Arthur Rimbaud: portraits, dessins, manuscrits,*
   RMN, Paris, 1991

Etiemble, René, *le Mythe de Rimbaud* (5 vols), Gallimard, Paris, 1954 et seq.

   Le Sonnet des Voyelles, Gallimard, Paris 1968

Etiemble et Yassu Gayclère, *Rimbaud,* Gallimard, Paris, 1936

Fongaro, Antoine, *Sur Rimbaud. Lire 'Illuminations',* Université de Toulouse Le Mirail,
   coll. Littératures, 1985

Forestier, Louis, *Charles Cros, L'Homme et l'oeuvre,* Lettres modernes, Minard,
   Paris, 1969

Gimpel, René, *Journal d'un Collectionneur-Marchand de Tableaux,* Hachette, Paris, 1963
   (*Diary of an Art Dealer,* trans. John Rosenberg, FSG, New York, 1966)

Giusto, Jean-Pierre 'Verlaine-Rimbaud ...', in *Parade Sauvage: revue d'études
   rimbaldiennes,* vol. 3, April 1986

Colonel Godchot, *Arthur Rimbaud ne varietur,* Slatkine reprints,
   Geneva, 1983 (original edition, 1936–7)

Goffin, Robert, *Rimbaud Vivant,* Corrêa, Paris, 1937

   Rimbaud et Verlaine Vivants, L'Ecran du Monde, Paris, 1948

Guyaux, André, *Poétique du fragment. Essai sur les Illuminations.*
   La Baconnière, Neuchâtel, 1986

Hackett, Cecil, *Rimbaud,* Bowes and Bowes, London, 1957

   Autour de Rimbaud, Klinckseick, Paris, 1967

   Rimbaud: a Critical Introduction, Cambridge University Press, Cambridge, 1981

Ibrovac, Modrag, *José-Maria de Heredia: sa vie, son oeuvre,* Les Presses françaises, Paris, 1923

Izambard, Georges, *Rimbaud Tel que je l'ai connu,* Mercure de France, Paris, 1946

James, Henry, 'A Little Tour of France' in *Collected Travel Writing,*
   Library of America, New York, 1993

Lefrère, Jean-Jacques and Pakenham, Michael, *Cabaner, poète au piano,*
   L'échoppe, Paris, 1994

Little, Roger, *Rimbaud. Illuminations,* Grant and Cutler, London, 1983

Macé, Gérard, 'Rimbaud Recently Deserted', in *Ex Libris*, Gallimard, Paris, 1987

Mallarmé, Stéphane, *Oeuvres complètes*, eds Henri Mondor and G-J Aubry, Gallimard, Bibliothèque de la Pléiade, Paris, 1951

Matarasso, Henri and Petitfils, Pierre, *Album Rimbaud,* Gallimard, Paris, 1967

Miannay, Régis, *Maurice Rollinat: poète et musicien du Fantastique,* presses de l'imprimerie Badel, Sautron, 1981

Miller, Henry, *The Time of the Assassins*, New Directions, New York, 1956

Mouquet, Jules, *Rimbaud raconté par Paul Verlaine*, Mercure de France, Paris, 1934

Murphy, Steve, 'Rimbaud et la Commune?' in *Rimbaud Multiple: Colloque de Cerisy,* eds Bedou and Touzot,Gordon and Paris, 1986

'Contre les 'Derniers vers' in *Arthur Rimbaud: Poesia e Avventura*, Pacini ed., Pisa, 1987

'Illuminations obscures – singularités sémantiques', in *Rimbaud: le poème en prose,* ed. Sergio Sacchi, Gunter Narr Verlag, Tübingen, 1988

Le Premier Rimbaud ou l'apprentissage de la subversion, ed. CNRS, Paris, 1990

Rimbaud et la ménagerie impériale, Presses universitaires de Lyon, ed. CNRS, Lyon, 1991

(ed.) *Arthur Rimbaud, Un Coeur sous une soutane*, Musée Rimbaud, Charleville-Mézières, 1991

'Le roman de vivre à deux hommes: Rimbaud et Verlaine', in *Dédicaces à Paul Verlaine*, ed. Serpenoise, Metz, 1996

Petitfils, Pierre, *Rimbaud,* Julliard, Paris 1982 (trans. Alan Sheridan, University of Virginia Press, Charlottesville, 1987)

L'Oeuvre et le visage d'Arthur Rimbaud, Nizet, Paris, 1949

Rimbaud au fil des ans 1854–1984, ed. Musée-Bibliothèque Rimbaud, Charleville-Mézières, 1984

Peyre, Henri, *Rimbaud vu par Verlaine,* Nizet, Paris, 1975

La Littérature Symboliste, PUF Que sais-je? Paris, 1976

Pia, Pascal (ed.), *l'Album zutique,* Jean-Jacques Pauvert, Paris, 1962

Ponchon, Raoul, *La Muse au cabaret,* bibliothèque Charpentier, Paris, 1920

Puget, Jean, *La vie extraordinaire de Forain*, Paris, 1957

Richepin, Jean, *Truandailles*, bibliothèque Charpentier, Paris, 1891

Grandes amoureuses, bibliothèque Charpentier, Paris, 1896

'Toutes mes vies. Des copains. Pages d'album.' in *Demain*, vol. 13, April 1925

Rimbaud, Isabelle, *Reliques*, Mercure de France, Paris, 1921

Rimbaud, cent ans après. Acts of a Rimbaud centennial colloqium, Musée Rimbaud, Charleville-Mézières, 1991

Risset, Jacqueline, 'Une Saison au Paradis: Rimbaud lecteur de Dante', in *Quaderni del seminario di filologia francese* , vol. 1, 1993, pp. 117–127

Robertson, William John, *A Century of French Verse*, AD Innes & Co, London, 1895
Ruchon, François, *Rimbaud, Documents iconographiques*, P. Caillier,
    Vesenaz-Geneva, 1946
Starkie, Enid, *Arthur Rimbaud*, New Directions, New York, 1962
Steinmetz, Jean-Luc, 'Rimbaud et le Faust de Goethe', in *Dix études sur Une Saison en Enfer*, ed. André Guyaux, Ed. de la Baconnière, Paris, 1994
    Rimbaud, Une question de Présence, Tallandier, Paris, 1995
Sutton, Howard, *The Life and Work of Jean Richepin*, Librairie Droz, Geneva, 1961
Underwood, Vernon, *Rimbaud et l'Angleterre*, Nizet, Paris 1976
Vaillat, Léandre, *En Ecoutant Forain*, Paris, 1931
Voellmy, Jean, 'Rimbaud par ceux qui l'ont connu', in *Parade Sauvage*, Charleville-Mézières, 1992.
Walzer, Pierre-Olivier, ed. Lautréamont, *Germain Nouveau, Oeuvres complètes*,
    Gallimard Bibliothèque de la Pléiade, Paris, 1970

On Verlaine

Buisine, Alain, *Paul Verlaine: Histoire d'un Corps*, Tallandier, Paris, 1995
Cazals, F.A. and Le Rouge, Gustave, *Les Derniers Jours de Paul Verlaine*,
    Mercure de France, Paris, 1923
Copeau, Jacques, *Journal 1901–1948, vol. I ,1905–1915*, ed. Claude Sicard, Seghers, Paris, 1991
Coulon, Marcel, *Verlaine poète saturnien*, Grasset, Paris, 1929 (trans. Edgell Rickword as *Poet Under Saturn: The Tragedy of Verlaine*, H. Toulmin, London, 1932)
Delahaye, Ernest, *Verlaine*, Messein, Paris, 1919
    Documents relatifs à Paul Verlaine, Maison du livre, Paris, 1919
Drillon, Jacques (ed.), *Tombeau de Verlaine*, Le Promeneur, Gallimard, Paris, 1995
Ellis, Havelock, 'The Approach to Verlaine', in *From Rousseau to Proust*, Houghton Mifflin, New York, 1935
Frémy, Yann, 'en dehors des Romances', in *Revue Verlaine*, vols 3–4, 1996
Hanson, Lawrence and Elisabeth, *Verlaine: Prince of Poets*, Chatto & Windus, London, 1958
Hart-Davis, Rupert (ed.), *The Letters of Oscar Wilde*, Harcourt Brace, New York, 1962
Lalande, Françoise, 'L'Examen corporel d'un homme de lettres', in *Parade Sauvage: revue d'études rimbaldiennes*, vol. 2, April 1985
Lee, Joon-Oh (ed.), *Arthur Rimbaud et Paul Verlaine – Comme les poètes maudits*, Presses de l'Université de Soong-Sil, Korea, 1996

Lepelletier, Edmond, *Paul Verlaine, sa vie, son oeuvre*, Mercure de France, Paris, 1923

Mauté, Mathilde (ex-Madame Paul Verlaine), *Mémoires de ma Vie*, Flammarion, Paris, 1935 (new edition prefaced and annotated by Michael Pakenham, Champ Vallon, Paris, 1992)

Nicholson, Harold, *Paul Verlaine*, Constable, London, 1921

Petitfils, Pierre, *Album Verlaine*, Gallimard, Paris, 1981

Peyré, Yves (ed.), *Dédicaces à Paul Verlaine*, Serpenoise, Metz, 1996

Régamey, Félix, *Verlaine dessinateur*, H. Flory, Paris, 1896

Richardson, Joanna, *Verlaine*, Weidenfeld & Nicholson, London, 1971

Ruchon, François, *Verlaine: Documents iconographiques*, P. Cailler, Geneva, 1947

Sherard, Robert Harborough, *Twenty Years in Paris: Being Some Recollections of a Literary Life*, Hutchinson, London, 1906

Underwood, Vernon, *Verlaine et l'Angleterre*, Nizet, Paris, 1956

Verlaine, Paul, *Correspondence*, ed. Ad. van Bever, 3 vols, Messein, Paris, 1922–1929
    Femmes/Hombres, ed. Jean-Paul Corsetti and Jean-Pierre Giusto, *Le Livre à Venir*, Paris, 1985 (revised edition 1990 from Terrain vague, 'le bleu du ciel')

Vial, André, *Verlaine et les Siens: Heures Retrouvées*, Librairie A., Nizet, Paris, 1975

Zayed, Georges, *La Formation littéraire de Verlaine*, Droz, Geneva, 1970
    (ed.) *Lettres inédites de Verlaine à Cazals*, Droz, Geneva, 1957
    (ed.) *Paul Verlaine, Lettres inédites à Charles Morice*, Droz, Geneva, 1969
    (ed.) *Paul Verlaine, Lettres inédites à divers correspondants*, Droz, Geneva, 1976

Zweig, Stefan, *Paul Verlaine*, trans. O.F. Theis, Luce, Boston 1913

On Rimbaud's influence

Berger, Anne-Emmanuelle, *Le Banquet de Rimbaud. Récherches sur l'oralité*, Champ Vallon, Paris, 1992

Billot, Marcel (ed.), *Journal de l'Abbé Mugnier (1879–1939)*, Mercure de France, Paris, 1985

Bloy, Léon, *Oeuvres de Léon Bloy*, vol. 15, Mercure de France, Paris, 1975

Brecht, Bertolt, *Journale I, 1913–1941*, Aufbau-verlag, Berlin and Weimar, 1994

Butor, Michel, *Improvisations sur Rimbaud*, La Différence, Paris, 1989
    Cahiers Jean Cocteau 2, Jean Cocteau et Anne de Noailles, Correspondance, Gallimard, Paris, 1989
    Cahiers Jean Cocteau 12, Correspondance avec Jacques Maritain, Gallimard, Paris, 1993

Carpenter, Humphrey, *Benjamin Britten*, Faber, London, 1992

Cioran, E.M., *Cahiers 1957–1972*, Gallimard, Paris, 1997

Claudel, Paul and Gide, André, *Correspondance 1899–1926*, Gallimard, Paris, 1949

Crevel, René, *Lettres de Désir et de souffrance*, Fayard, Paris, 1996

Dalven, Rae, *A Season in Hell: a play*, produced in New York, 1950 (unpublished, lost?)

Fowlie, Wallace, *Rimbaud and Jim Morrison: the Rebel as Poet*, Duke University Press, Durham, 1993

Fuegi, John, *Brecht & Company*, Grove Press, New York, 1994

George, Stefan, *Zeitgenössische Dichter*, Georg Bondi, Berlin, 1905

Gibson, Ian, *Federico Garcia Lorca, a Life*, Pantheon, New York, 1989

Gide, André, *Journal*, Gallimard, Paris, 1969

Ginsberg, Allen, *Allen Verbatim*, McGraw Hill, New York, 1974

Guyaux, André, 'Jean Cocteau et le premier des "enfants terribles"', in *Parade Sauvage Colloque No. 2*, Charleville, 1987

Hare, Humphrey, *Sketch for a Portrait of Rimbaud*, Brendin Publishing, London, 1937

Harpprecht, Klaus, *Thomas Mann: Eine Biographie*, Rowohlt, Berlin, 1995

Hayes, Deborah, *Peggy Glanville-Hicks, a bio-bibliography*, Greenwood Press, New York, 1990

Harris, Frank, *Contemporary Portraits*, Mitchell Kennerly, New York, 1915

Harvey, Andrew, *The Essential Gay Mystics*, HarperSanfrancisco, San Francisco, 1997

Henze, Hans Werner, *Hans Werner Henze, a catalogue of his work*, Schott, Mainz, 1996

Jacob, Max, *Lettres à Liane de Pougy*, Plon, Paris, 1980

   Lettres à Marcel Jouhandeau, Librairie Droz, Geneva, 1979

   Les Propos et les Jours, Zodiaques, 1989

Jouhandeau, Marcel, *Journaliers V, IX, X, XI, XXI, XXII*, Gallimard, Paris, 1963–1973

Kavanagh, Julie, *Secret Muses: the Life of Frederick Ashton*, Pantheon, New York, 1996

Landmann, Edith, *Gespräche mit Stefan George*, Helmut Küpper, Dusseldorf, 1963

Léautaud, Paul, *Journal Littéraire, vols II, IX, X*, Mercure de France, Paris, 1952–1964

Mann, Klaus, *Briefe und Antworten Band I 1922–1937*, ed. Martin Gregor-Dullin, Spangenberg Publishers, Munich, 1975

   Tagebücher, vols 2, 4, 5, ed. Spangenberg Publishers, Munich, 1994

Mauriac, François *Bloc-notes*, (5 vols), ed. Seuil, Paris, 1993

Miles, Barry, *Ginsberg: a Biography*, Simon & Schuster, New York, 1989

Moore, George, *Impressions and Opinions*, Scribner, New York, 1891

   Memoirs of My Dead Life, Appleton, New York, 1906

Moraly, Jean-Bernard, *Jean Genet: La Vie Ecrite*, La Différence, Paris, 1988

Morrissette, Bruce, *The Great Rimbaud Forgery: The Affair of La Chasse Spirituelle*, Washington University Studies, St Louis, 1956

Nicholl, Charles, *Somebody Else: Arthur Rimbaud in Africa 1880–1891*, Cape, London, 1996

Noël, Jean C., *George Moore l'homme et l'oeuvre (1852–1933)*, Didier, Paris, 1966

Palmer, Christopher, *The Britten Companion,* Cambridge University Press, 1984

Pasolini, Pier Paolo, *Letters,* Nico Naldini, trans. Stuart Hood, Quartet Books, London, 1992

Penna, Sandro, *Poesie scelte,* Einaudi, Torino, 1984

Le Pont de l'Epée, vol. 76, September 1982; special issue, 'La chasse spirituelle et la critique'

Marcel Proust, *Correspondance vol. XVII, XIX,* ed. Philip Kolb, Plon, Paris, 1980

Raczymow, Henry, *Maurice Sachs ou les travaux forcés de la frivolité,* Gallimard, Paris, 1988

Reed, Jeremy, *Delirium: an Interpretation of Arthur Rimbaud,* Peter Owen, London, 1991

Restagno, Enzo, *Henze,* EDT ed., Turin, 1986

Retté, Adolphe, *Le Symbolisme: anecdotes et souvenirs*, Librairie Léon Vanier, Paris, 1903
   Quand L'Esprit Souffle: Récits de Conversion - Huysmans, Verlaine, Claudel..., ed. Messein, Paris, 1914

Richardson, Joanna, *Enid Starkie: a biography,* Macmillan, London, 1973

van Rogger-Andreucci, Christine, *Poésie et Réligion dans l'oeuvre de Max Jacob*, Honoré Champion, Paris, 1994

Russell, Charles, *Poets, Prophets, and Revolutionaries: the Literary Avant-Garde from Rimbaud through Postmodernism,* Oxford University Press, 1985

Sackville-West, Edward, *The Apology of Arthur Rimbaud: a Dialogue,* Hogarth Essays, no. 7, London, 1927

Sartre, Jean-Paul, *Le Mur,* Gallimard, Paris, 1939

Schifano, Laurence, trans. Byron, William, *Luchino Visconti: the flames of passion,* Collins, London, 1990

Segalen, Victor, *Le Double Rimbaud,* Fata Morgana, Paris, 1979

Sénac, Jean, *Dérisions et Vertiges: Trouvures,* Actes Sud, Arles, 1983
   Poésie au Sud: Jean Sénac et la nouvelle poésie algérienne, archives de la ville de Marseille, 1983

Strachey, Lytton, *Eminent Victorians,* Chatto & Windus, London, 1918

Unterecker, John, *Voyager: a Life of Hart Crane,* FSG, New York, 1969

Wojnarowicz, David, *Brush Fires in the Social Landscape,* Aperture, New York, 1994

Yourcenar, Marguerite, *Lettres à ses amis et quelques autres,* Gallimard, Paris 1995

Picture Credits

Cover photograph & Pg. 6	From the collection of Roger Lathbury
All other images	Courtesy of the Rimbaud Museum, Charleville-Mézières

Index